THE BOOK
OF PROVERBS

THE BOOK
OF PROVERBS

from the Authorized King James Version
with an introduction by Robert Gordis and
decorations by Valenti Angelo

THE HERITAGE PRESS
New York

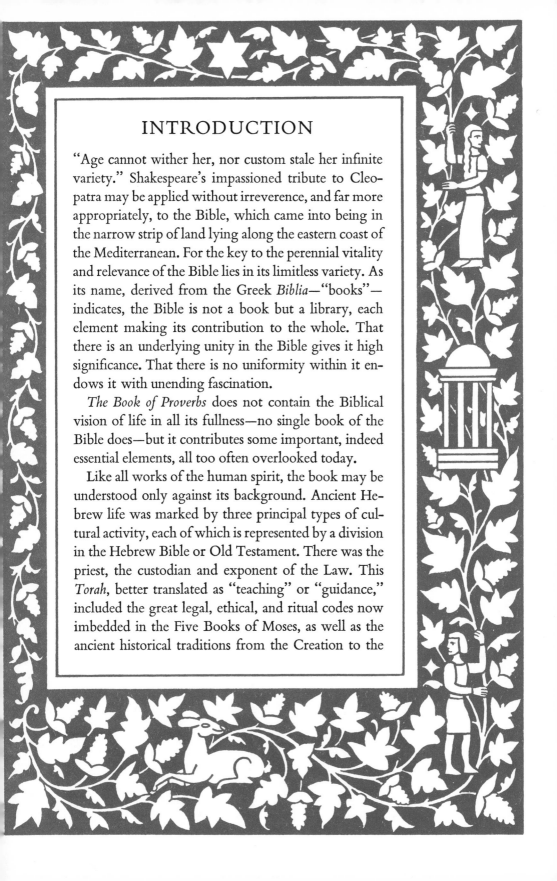

INTRODUCTION

"Age cannot wither her, nor custom stale her infinite variety." Shakespeare's impassioned tribute to Cleopatra may be applied without irreverence, and far more appropriately, to the Bible, which came into being in the narrow strip of land lying along the eastern coast of the Mediterranean. For the key to the perennial vitality and relevance of the Bible lies in its limitless variety. As its name, derived from the Greek *Biblia*—"books"—indicates, the Bible is not a book but a library, each element making its contribution to the whole. That there is an underlying unity in the Bible gives it high significance. That there is no uniformity within it endows it with unending fascination.

The Book of Proverbs does not contain the Biblical vision of life in all its fullness—no single book of the Bible does—but it contributes some important, indeed essential elements, all too often overlooked today.

Like all works of the human spirit, the book may be understood only against its background. Ancient Hebrew life was marked by three principal types of cultural activity, each of which is represented by a division in the Hebrew Bible or Old Testament. There was the priest, the custodian and exponent of the Law. This *Torah*, better translated as "teaching" or "guidance," included the great legal, ethical, and ritual codes now imbedded in the Five Books of Moses, as well as the ancient historical traditions from the Creation to the

death of Moses the Lawgiver. The priest based his authority on the Divine Revelation at Sinai, where the Law had been proclaimed to Moses and the assembled hosts of Israel.

Paralleling the priestly activity, and often in vigorous opposition to it, was the work of the Prophets. While they differed with regard to the value and importance of ritual, they were as one in emphasizing the primacy of righteousness. Mercy and justice were the Divine imperatives for man, and, by that token, the touchstone for judging the worth and permanence of any society. In Isaiah's words: "The result of justice shall be peace, and the reward of justice, quiet and security for ever." The source and sanction of the Prophets lay in no ancient revelation nor in any written document from the past. They had an overpowering sense of God's presence in the present. It was in His name that they spoke, and His will that they proclaimed, when they declared, "Thus saith the Lord."

For all the striking divergencies between them, both the Law and the Prophets placed the nation in the center of their thinking. Both were concerned with the weal or woe of the people as a whole, depending on whether or not it fulfilled the will of God, which the priest found embodied in the Law and the prophet in the moral code.

Nonetheless, the individual could not be disregarded. His personal happiness and success, his fears and his hopes, were by no means identical with the status of the nation. The people as a whole might be prosperous and happy, while the individual might be exposed to misery. On the other hand, even if the nation experienced defeat and subjugation to foreign masters, the individual could still adjust himself to conditions and extract at least a modicum of happiness and success from his environment.

It was the third strand of Hebrew culture, that of Wisdom, which made the life of the individual its primary concern. The connotations of the Hebrew term *Hokmah* are far wider than the English rendering "Wisdom" would imply. *Hokmah* may be defined as a realistic approach to the problems of life, including all the practical skills and the technical arts of civilization. These included not only the conduct of government and economic affairs, including such crafts as architecture, tapestry weaving, and sailing the sea, but also the composition and rendering of poetry and music. It encompassed the interpretation of dreams and the practice of magic. In Rabbinic Hebrew, the term was applied also to the midwife, upon whose skillful ministrations life and death depended.

What has remained of Biblical Wisdom today is its literary incarnations, which are concerned not so much with the arts of living as with developing a sane, workable attitude toward life. Unlike the priests and the prophets, the teachers of Wisdom, by and large, laid no claim to Divine Revelation, whether embodied in tradition or in direct communication. The credentials

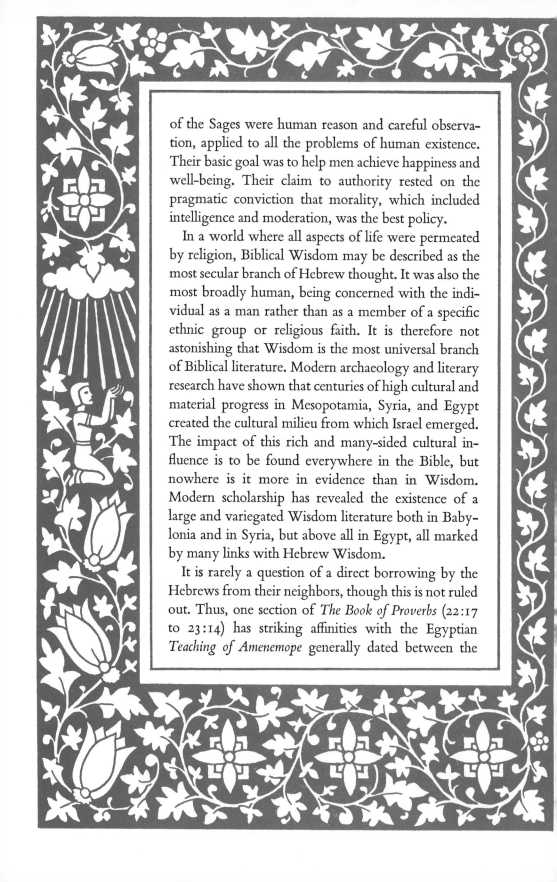

of the Sages were human reason and careful observation, applied to all the problems of human existence. Their basic goal was to help men achieve happiness and well-being. Their claim to authority rested on the pragmatic conviction that morality, which included intelligence and moderation, was the best policy.

In a world where all aspects of life were permeated by religion, Biblical Wisdom may be described as the most secular branch of Hebrew thought. It was also the most broadly human, being concerned with the individual as a man rather than as a member of a specific ethnic group or religious faith. It is therefore not astonishing that Wisdom is the most universal branch of Biblical literature. Modern archaeology and literary research have shown that centuries of high cultural and material progress in Mesopotamia, Syria, and Egypt created the cultural milieu from which Israel emerged. The impact of this rich and many-sided cultural influence is to be found everywhere in the Bible, but nowhere is it more in evidence than in Wisdom. Modern scholarship has revealed the existence of a large and variegated Wisdom literature both in Babylonia and in Syria, but above all in Egypt, all marked by many links with Hebrew Wisdom.

It is rarely a question of a direct borrowing by the Hebrews from their neighbors, though this is not ruled out. Thus, one section of *The Book of Proverbs* (22:17 to 23:14) has striking affinities with the Egyptian *Teaching of Amenemope* generally dated between the tenth and seventh centuries B.C. By and large, however, Biblical Wisdom—like its Sumerian, Syrian, Babylonian, and Egyptian counterparts—drew upon the common treasure-house of Wisdom which constituted part of the cultural background of the ancient Near East.

Traditionally, Hebrew Wisdom as a whole and *The Book of Proverbs* in particular are ascribed to King Solomon. Today, this Solomonic tradition is no longer airily dismissed by scholars as a figment of the folk-imagination. There is every reason to believe that Solomon's era marked the first Golden Age of Wisdom literature. His extensive contacts, political and commercial, with other countries, especially with Egypt, the domestic prosperity and sense of national well-being during his reign, and the existence of an extensive Wisdom literature in Egypt surely served as a spur to Hebrew creativity even if not as a source for emulation.

That Solomon himself engaged in literary composition is doubtful. Royal authors have been few and far between, Marcus Aurelius and Frederick the Great of Prussia being rare exceptions to the rule. Here, too, Egyptian Wisdom suggests the source of the tradition. Scribes were accustomed to attribute their writings to the king under whom they worked and, in fact, put words into the king's mouth. The common use of the phrase, "the King James Bible," to refer to the version produced during his reign, is a modern illustration of this practice.

To convey its truths, Wisdom created an educational

method in the form of academies or schools. These schools were frequented by young men, scions of the upper classes, the merchant princes, the large land-owners, the government officials. Here the Wisdom teachers sought to prepare their pupils for the responsibilities of family life, the conduct of business, and the administration of government.

The virtues that the Hebrew sages sought to inculcate were hard work, zeal, prudence, reliability, loyalty to authority, and religious conformity—all the elements of a morality making for worldly success. Where, however, ethical imperatives ran counter to more mundane considerations, they did not hesitate to urge less positive virtues on their youthful charges, such as holding one's tongue or distributing largesse, as aids in making one's way. Not only are vices dangerous; some virtues can be, too. The sages, therefore, warned their pupils not only against the vices of sexual license and drunkenness, but also against the virtue of going surety for the loans of others. In brief, this practical Wisdom represented a hard-headed, matter-of-fact, "safe and sane" approach to the problems of living.

The Wisdom teachers also developed a literature, with a characteristic genre all their own. It was the *Mashal*, which literally means "comparison" or "analogy." The term developed the basic connotation of "proverb" and from it the derived senses of "parable" and "allegory." Sometimes the single utterance might be extended into a short essay. But always the emphasis was upon pithiness of expression and aptness of illustration. In Biblical literature, the line of demarcation between prose and poetry is very slight. Biblical Wisdom tended to express itself in rhythmic forms, so that both the single proverb and the extended maxim are couched in verse rather than in prose.

Everywhere, the ancient Wisdom teachers upheld morality because they were convinced that it was a more effective road to success than sin. They preached adherence to religion because of the same pragmatic viewpoint: it served to make men good, and by that token, happy. In Israel the Prophets had stressed the ethical emphasis in religion, and their impact could not be ignored. The Wisdom teacher, therefore, identified Wisdom with virtue—the sinner is a fool and only he who is righteous and God-fearing is wise. This recognition of intelligence as a moral virtue and of folly as sin, is a fundamental insight of Wisdom thought. It is all too often lost sight of today, in discussions of the relevance of Biblical ethics to the practical life of the individual or to politics in the life of society. In no invidious sense, this school of Wisdom teachers may be described as the *lower* or *practical Wisdom*. Its great literary documents are *The Book of Proverbs* in the Bible and the later *Ecclesiasticus*, which is part of the Apocrypha but not the canon of Scripture.

Not all the Wisdom teachers were content to limit themselves to the earth-bound task of preparing young men for successful careers. There were some whose

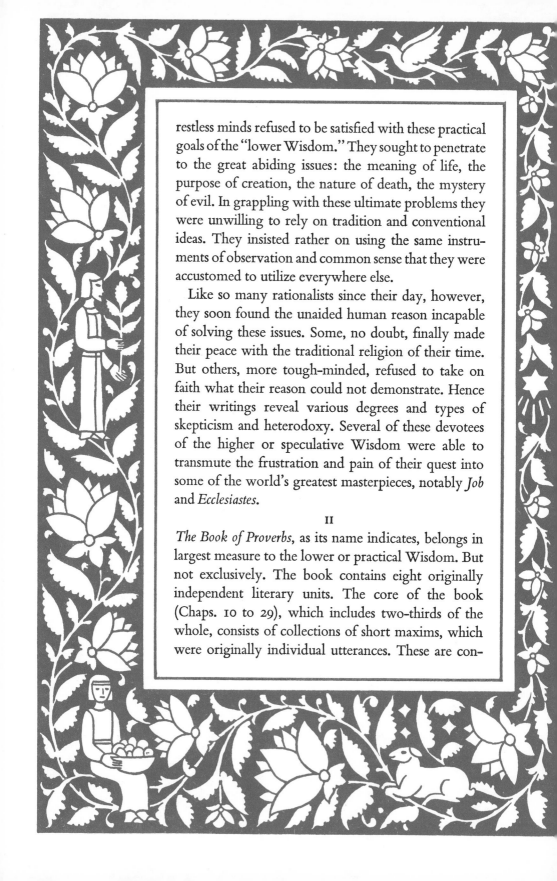

restless minds refused to be satisfied with these practical goals of the "lower Wisdom." They sought to penetrate to the great abiding issues: the meaning of life, the purpose of creation, the nature of death, the mystery of evil. In grappling with these ultimate problems they were unwilling to rely on tradition and conventional ideas. They insisted rather on using the same instruments of observation and common sense that they were accustomed to utilize everywhere else.

Like so many rationalists since their day, however, they soon found the unaided human reason incapable of solving these issues. Some, no doubt, finally made their peace with the traditional religion of their time. But others, more tough-minded, refused to take on faith what their reason could not demonstrate. Hence their writings reveal various degrees and types of skepticism and heterodoxy. Several of these devotees of the higher or speculative Wisdom were able to transmute the frustration and pain of their quest into some of the world's greatest masterpieces, notably *Job* and *Ecclesiastes*.

II

The Book of Proverbs, as its name indicates, belongs in largest measure to the lower or practical Wisdom. But not exclusively. The book contains eight originally independent literary units. The core of the book (Chaps. 10 to 29), which includes two-thirds of the whole, consists of collections of short maxims, which were originally individual utterances. These are con-

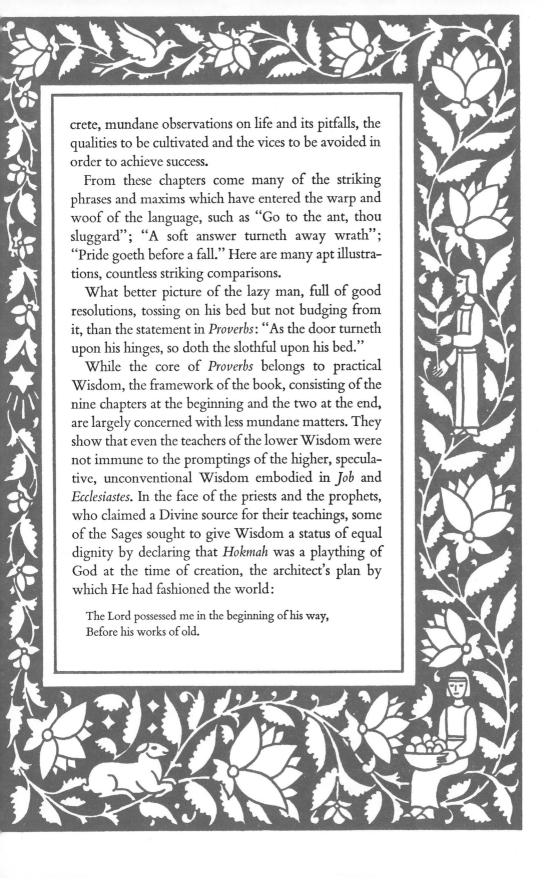

crete, mundane observations on life and its pitfalls, the qualities to be cultivated and the vices to be avoided in order to achieve success.

From these chapters come many of the striking phrases and maxims which have entered the warp and woof of the language, such as "Go to the ant, thou sluggard"; "A soft answer turneth away wrath"; "Pride goeth before a fall." Here are many apt illustrations, countless striking comparisons.

What better picture of the lazy man, full of good resolutions, tossing on his bed but not budging from it, than the statement in *Proverbs*: "As the door turneth upon his hinges, so doth the slothful upon his bed."

While the core of *Proverbs* belongs to practical Wisdom, the framework of the book, consisting of the nine chapters at the beginning and the two at the end, are largely concerned with less mundane matters. They show that even the teachers of the lower Wisdom were not immune to the promptings of the higher, speculative, unconventional Wisdom embodied in *Job* and *Ecclesiastes*. In the face of the priests and the prophets, who claimed a Divine source for their teachings, some of the Sages sought to give Wisdom a status of equal dignity by declaring that *Hokmah* was a plaything of God at the time of creation, the architect's plan by which He had fashioned the world:

> The Lord possessed me in the beginning of his way,
> Before his works of old.

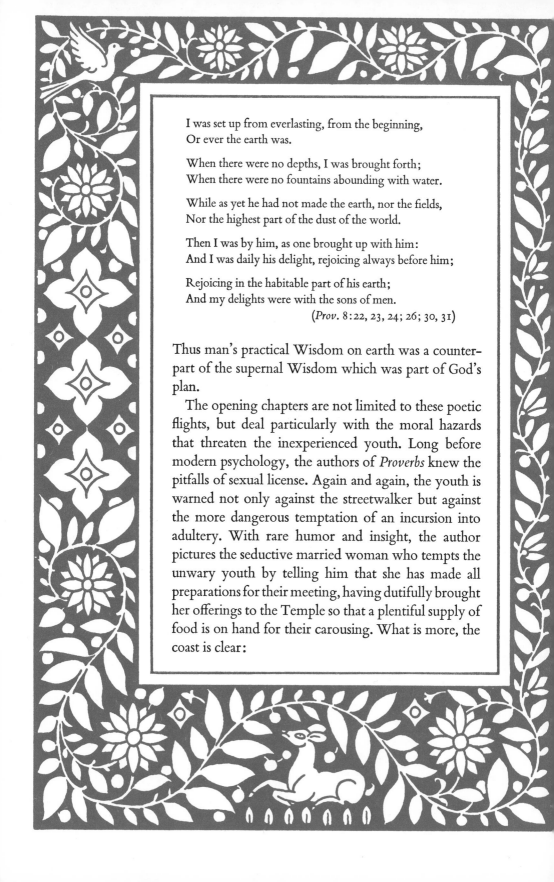

I was set up from everlasting, from the beginning,
Or ever the earth was.

When there were no depths, I was brought forth;
When there were no fountains abounding with water.

While as yet he had not made the earth, nor the fields,
Nor the highest part of the dust of the world.

Then I was by him, as one brought up with him:
And I was daily his delight, rejoicing always before him;

Rejoicing in the habitable part of his earth;
And my delights were with the sons of men.

(Prov. 8:22, 23, 24; 26; 30, 31)

Thus man's practical Wisdom on earth was a counterpart of the supernal Wisdom which was part of God's plan.

The opening chapters are not limited to these poetic flights, but deal particularly with the moral hazards that threaten the inexperienced youth. Long before modern psychology, the authors of *Proverbs* knew the pitfalls of sexual license. Again and again, the youth is warned not only against the streetwalker but against the more dangerous temptation of an incursion into adultery. With rare humor and insight, the author pictures the seductive married woman who tempts the unwary youth by telling him that she has made all preparations for their meeting, having dutifully brought her offerings to the Temple so that a plentiful supply of food is on hand for their carousing. What is more, the coast is clear:

For the goodman is not at home, he is gone a long journey:
He hath taken a bag of money with him, and will come
   home at the day appointed.   (*Prov.* 7:19, 20)

But the doom of the sinner is certain:

For she hath cast down many wounded: yea, many strong
   men have been slain by her.
Her house is the way to hell, going down to the chambers
   of death.   (*Prov.* 7:26, 27)

As against these debasements of love, the Wisdom teacher, in words of moving beauty, urges loyalty to the wife of one's youth:

      Drink waters out of thine own cistern,
      And running waters out of thine own well.
      Let thy fountain be blessed;
      And rejoice with the wife of thy youth.
               (*Prov.* 5:15, 18)

Just as men are divided by the Biblical sages into two categories, the wise man and the fool, women also belong to two great classes. The evil woman need not be guilty of sexual immorality; her vices may be less fundamental, but very trying, nevertheless—bad temper, quarrelsomeness, indolence, lack of sense. On the other hand, a good wife is the greatest mark of God's favor. The book concludes with a moving paean of praise to "the virtuous woman," wise, resourceful, energetic, looking well to the ways of her household, but also engaging in business ventures, while her husband is honored among the elders in the gate. The ideal

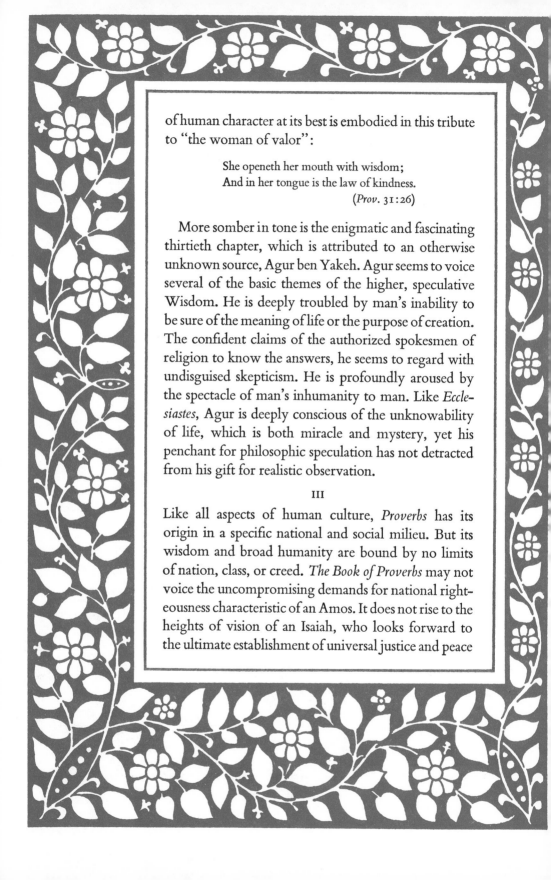

of human character at its best is embodied in this tribute to "the woman of valor":

> She openeth her mouth with wisdom;
> And in her tongue is the law of kindness.
> (*Prov.* 31:26)

More somber in tone is the enigmatic and fascinating thirtieth chapter, which is attributed to an otherwise unknown source, Agur ben Yakeh. Agur seems to voice several of the basic themes of the higher, speculative Wisdom. He is deeply troubled by man's inability to be sure of the meaning of life or the purpose of creation. The confident claims of the authorized spokesmen of religion to know the answers, he seems to regard with undisguised skepticism. He is profoundly aroused by the spectacle of man's inhumanity to man. Like *Ecclesiastes*, Agur is deeply conscious of the unknowability of life, which is both miracle and mystery, yet his penchant for philosophic speculation has not detracted from his gift for realistic observation.

III

Like all aspects of human culture, *Proverbs* has its origin in a specific national and social milieu. But its wisdom and broad humanity are bound by no limits of nation, class, or creed. *The Book of Proverbs* may not voice the uncompromising demands for national righteousness characteristic of an Amos. It does not rise to the heights of vision of an Isaiah, who looks forward to the ultimate establishment of universal justice and peace among nations under the sovereignty of God's law. The pathos of Hosea, loving, betrayed, and loving still, and the agony of Jeremiah, doomed to proclaim the destruction of his people and to be hated for it, are poles apart from the sober reflections on everyday life by the authors of *Proverbs*. The Sages make no claim to the mystic fervor of the Psalmist or the profound passion of a Job.

Yet it would be a great mistake to dismiss the value of *Proverbs* and to overlook its unique blending of wisdom and charm, of insight and aspiration. For the generality of men, here and now, it offers a sane and workable morality, a guide against the perils and temptations of daily life. Its practical counsel is buttressed by the conviction that we live in a world created by God, who is the source of the Moral law, not only in its broad, universal sweep on the stage of history, but in its personal, immediate application to the life of Everyman. In an age of eroding moral standards, *The Book of Proverbs* cannot compel obedience. But it may persuade the minds and hearts of men to recognize that morality is not merely a system of police rules to be evaded with impunity, but a reflection of the basic laws of human existence.

Concerned basically with the individual, whose life is brief and whose goals are limited, the book nevertheless points to broader horizons as well. Rooted in the Wisdom tradition, *The Book of Proverbs* is far from hostile to the injunctions of the Law or the admonitions of

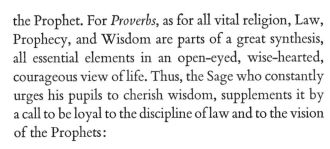

the Prophet. For *Proverbs*, as for all vital religion, Law, Prophecy, and Wisdom are parts of a great synthesis, all essential elements in an open-eyed, wise-hearted, courageous view of life. Thus, the Sage who constantly urges his pupils to cherish wisdom, supplements it by a call to be loyal to the discipline of law and to the vision of the Prophets:

> Where there is no vision, the people perish:
> But he that keepeth the law, happy is he.
> (*Prov.* 29:18)

It was the Hebrew Prophets who proclaimed the principle that the destiny of men and nations, for weal or woe, is determined by their adherence to the law of righteousness or their violation of it. Paradoxical as it may seem, the most succinct statement of this concept of history, perhaps the Prophets' greatest contribution to human thought, occurs not in the writings of Amos or Isaiah but in *The Book of Proverbs*:

> Righteousness exalteth a nation:
> But sin is a reproach to any people.
> (*Prov.* 14:34)

Thus the Biblical Wisdom teachers transmuted their realistic observations and practical common sense, through an act of faith, into a world-view. Thirty centuries later and under radically different circumstances, their vision of life still remains man's best hope of attaining to humanity.

ROBERT GORDIS

THE BOOK
OF PROVERBS

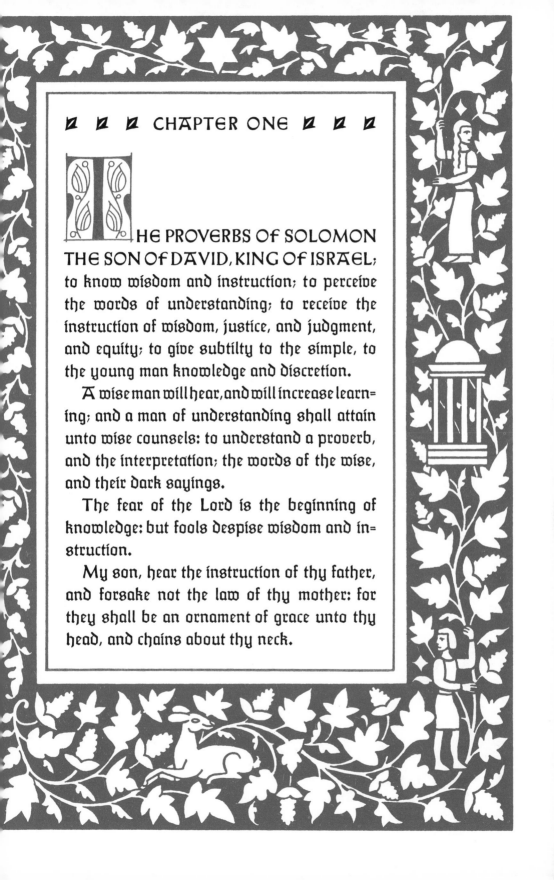

✠ ✠ ✠ CHAPTER ONE ✠ ✠ ✠

THE PROVERBS OF SOLOMON THE SON OF DAVID, KING OF ISRAEL; to know wisdom and instruction; to perceive the words of understanding; to receive the instruction of wisdom, justice, and judgment, and equity; to give subtilty to the simple, to the young man knowledge and discretion.

A wise man will hear, and will increase learn=ing; and a man of understanding shall attain unto wise counsels: to understand a proverb, and the interpretation; the words of the wise, and their dark sayings.

The fear of the Lord is the beginning of knowledge: but fools despise wisdom and in=struction.

My son, hear the instruction of thy father, and forsake not the law of thy mother: for they shall be an ornament of grace unto thy head, and chains about thy neck.

My son, if sinners entice thee, consent thou not. If they say, Come with us, let us lay wait for blood, let us lurk privily for the innocent without cause: let us swallow them up alive as the grave; and whole, as those that go down into the pit: we shall find all precious substance, we shall fill our houses with spoil: cast in thy lot among us; let us all have one purse: my son, walk not thou in the way with them; refrain thy foot from their path: for their feet run to evil, and make haste to shed blood.

Surely in vain the net is spread in the sight of any bird.

And they lay wait for their own blood; they lurk privily for their own lives.

So are the ways of every one that is greedy of gain; which taketh away the life of the owners thereof.

Wisdom crieth without; she uttereth her voice in the streets: she crieth in the chief place of concourse, in the openings of the gates: in the city she uttereth her words, saying, How long, ye simple ones, will ye love simplicity? and the scorners delight in their scorning, and fools

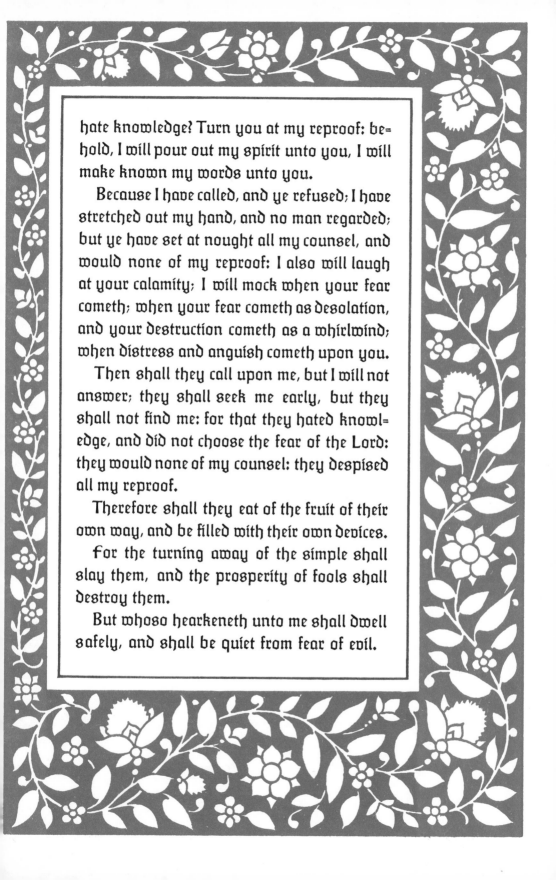

hate knowledge? Turn you at my reproof: behold, I will pour out my spirit unto you, I will make known my words unto you.

Because I have called, and ye refused; I have stretched out my hand, and no man regarded; but ye have set at nought all my counsel, and would none of my reproof: I also will laugh at your calamity; I will mock when your fear cometh; when your fear cometh as desolation, and your destruction cometh as a whirlwind; when distress and anguish cometh upon you.

Then shall they call upon me, but I will not answer; they shall seek me early, but they shall not find me: for that they hated knowledge, and did not choose the fear of the Lord: they would none of my counsel: they despised all my reproof.

Therefore shall they eat of the fruit of their own way, and be filled with their own devices.

For the turning away of the simple shall slay them, and the prosperity of fools shall destroy them.

But whoso hearkeneth unto me shall dwell safely, and shall be quiet from fear of evil.

CHAPTER TWO

MY SON, if thou wilt receive my words, and hide my commandments with thee; so that thou incline thine ear unto wisdom, and apply thine heart to understanding; yea, if thou criest after knowledge, and liftest up thy voice for understanding; if thou seekest her as silver, and searchest for her as for hid treas= ures; then shalt thou understand the fear of the Lord, and find the knowledge of God.

For the Lord giveth wisdom: out of his mouth cometh knowledge and understanding.

He layeth up sound wisdom for the right= eous: he is a buckler to them that walk uprightly.

He keepeth the paths of judgment, and pre= serveth the way of his saints.

Then shalt thou understand righteousness, and judgment, and equity; yea, every good path.

When wisdom entereth into thine heart, and knowledge is pleasant unto thy soul; discre=

tion shall preserve thee, understanding shall keep thee: to deliver thee from the way of the evil man, from the man that speaketh froward things; who leave the paths of uprightness, to walk in the ways of darkness; who rejoice to do evil, and delight in the frowardness of the wicked; whose ways are crooked, and they froward in their paths: to deliver thee from the strange woman, even from the stranger which flattereth with her words; which forsaketh the guide of her youth, and forgetteth the covenant of her God.

For her house inclineth unto death, and her paths unto the dead.

None that go unto her return again, neither take they hold of the paths of life.

That thou mayest walk in the way of good men, and keep the paths of the righteous.

For the upright shall dwell in the land, and the perfect shall remain in it.

But the wicked shall be cut off from the earth, and the transgressors shall be rooted out of it.

CHAPTER THREE

MY SON, forget not my law; but let thine heart keep my commandments: for length of days, and long life, and peace, shall they add to thee.

Let not mercy and truth forsake thee: bind them about thy neck; write them upon the table of thine heart: so shalt thou find favor and good understanding in the sight of God and man.

Trust in the Lord with all thine heart; and lean not unto thine own understanding.

In all thy ways acknowledge him, and he shall direct thy paths.

Be not wise in thine own eyes: fear the Lord, and depart from evil.

It shall be health to thy navel, and marrow to thy bones.

Honor the Lord with thy substance, and with the firstfruits of all thine increase: so shall thy barns be filled with plenty, and

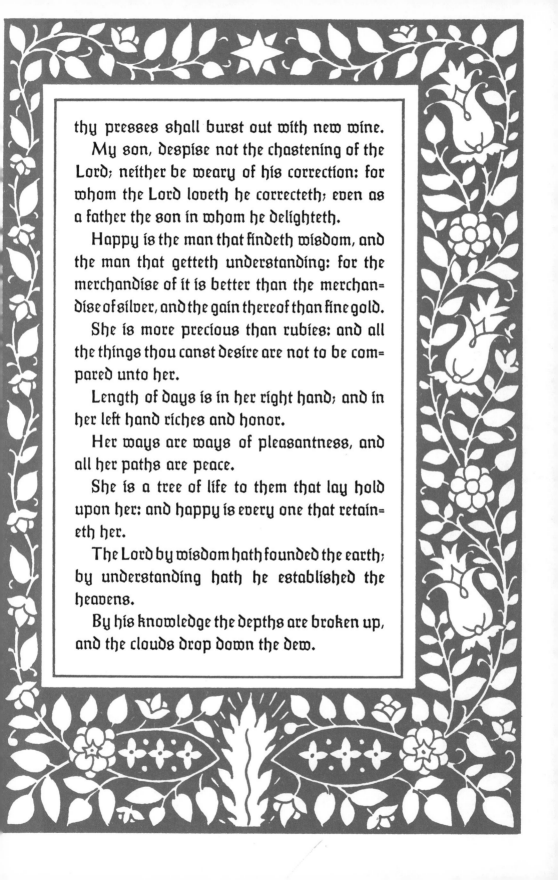

thy presses shall burst out with new wine.

My son, despise not the chastening of the Lord; neither be weary of his correction: for whom the Lord loveth he correcteth; even as a father the son in whom he delighteth.

Happy is the man that findeth wisdom, and the man that getteth understanding: for the merchandise of it is better than the merchandise of silver, and the gain thereof than fine gold.

She is more precious than rubies: and all the things thou canst desire are not to be compared unto her.

Length of days is in her right hand; and in her left hand riches and honor.

Her ways are ways of pleasantness, and all her paths are peace.

She is a tree of life to them that lay hold upon her: and happy is every one that retaineth her.

The Lord by wisdom hath founded the earth; by understanding hath he established the heavens.

By his knowledge the depths are broken up, and the clouds drop down the dew.

My son, let not them depart from thine eyes: keep sound wisdom and discretion: so shall they be life unto thy soul, and grace to thy neck.

Then shalt thou walk in thy way safely, and thy foot shall not stumble.

When thou liest down, thou shalt not be a=fraid: yea, thou shalt lie down, and thy sleep shall be sweet.

Be not afraid ot sudden fear, neither of the desolation of the wicked, when it cometh.

For the Lord shall be thy confidence, and shall keep thy foot from being taken.

Withhold not good from them to whom it is due, when it is in the power of thine hand to do it.

Say not unto thy neighbor, Go, and come again, and tomorrow I will give; when thou hast it by thee.

Devise not evil against thy neighbor, seeing he dwelleth securely by thee.

Strive not with a man without cause, if he have done thee no harm.

Envy thou not the oppressor, and choose none of his ways.

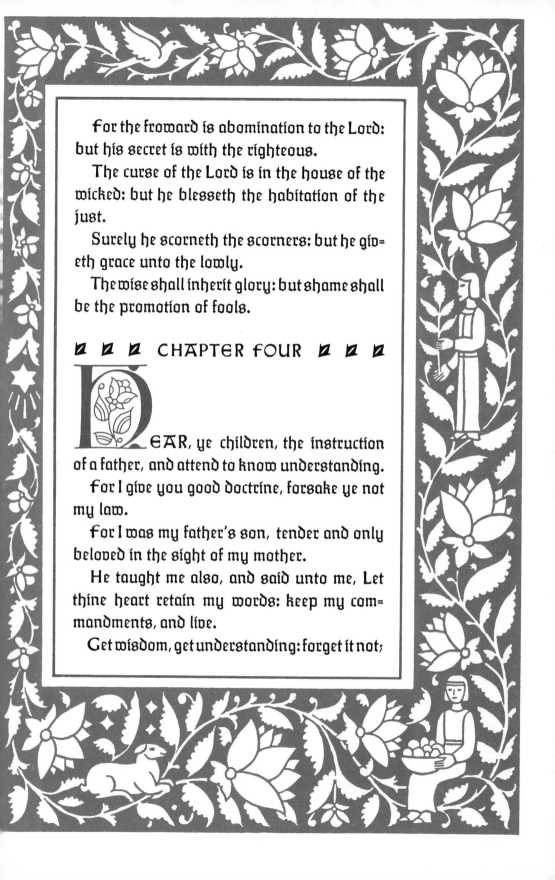

For the froward is abomination to the Lord: but his secret is with the righteous.

The curse of the Lord is in the house of the wicked: but he blesseth the habitation of the just.

Surely he scorneth the scorners: but he giveth grace unto the lowly.

The wise shall inherit glory: but shame shall be the promotion of fools.

⬧ ⬧ ⬧ CHAPTER FOUR ⬧ ⬧ ⬧

HEAR, ye children, the instruction of a father, and attend to know understanding.

For I give you good doctrine, forsake ye not my law.

For I was my father's son, tender and only beloved in the sight of my mother.

He taught me also, and said unto me, Let thine heart retain my words: keep my commandments, and live.

Get wisdom, get understanding: forget it not;

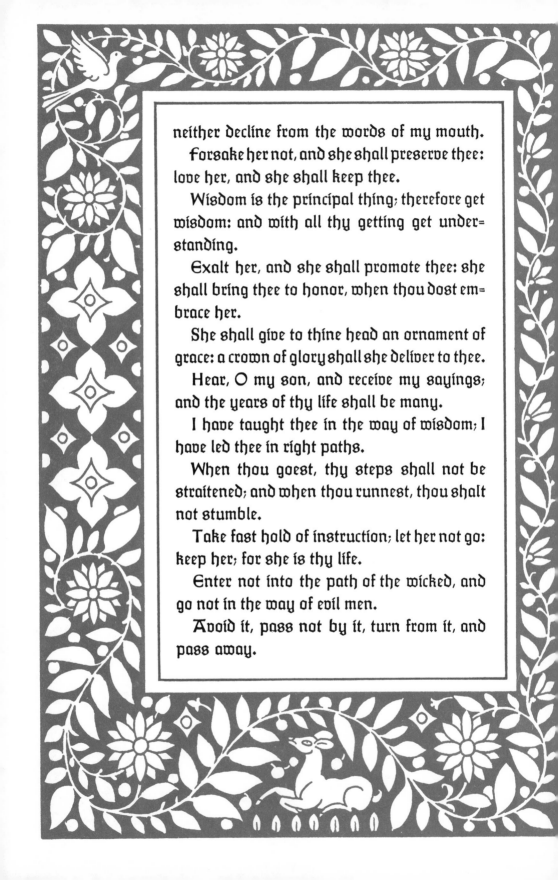

neither decline from the words of my mouth.

Forsake her not, and she shall preserve thee: love her, and she shall keep thee.

Wisdom is the principal thing; therefore get wisdom: and with all thy getting get understanding.

Exalt her, and she shall promote thee: she shall bring thee to honor, when thou dost embrace her.

She shall give to thine head an ornament of grace: a crown of glory shall she deliver to thee.

Hear, O my son, and receive my sayings; and the years of thy life shall be many.

I have taught thee in the way of wisdom; I have led thee in right paths.

When thou goest, thy steps shall not be straitened; and when thou runnest, thou shalt not stumble.

Take fast hold of instruction; let her not go: keep her; for she is thy life.

Enter not into the path of the wicked, and go not in the way of evil men.

Avoid it, pass not by it, turn from it, and pass away.

For they sleep not, except they have done mischief; and their sleep is taken away, unless they cause some to fall.

For they eat the bread of wickedness, and drink the wine of violence.

But the path of the just is as the shining light, that shineth more and more unto the perfect day.

The way of the wicked is as darkness: they know not at what they stumble.

My son, attend to my words; incline thine ear unto my sayings.

Let them not depart from thine eyes; keep them in the midst of thine heart.

For they are life unto those that find them, and health to all their flesh.

Keep thy heart with all diligence; for out of it are the issues of life.

Put away from thee a froward mouth, and perverse lips put far from thee.

Let thine eyes look right on, and let thine eyelids look straight before thee.

Ponder the path of thy feet, and let all thy ways be established.

Turn not to the right hand nor to the left: remove thy foot from evil.

◪ ◪ ◪ CHAPTER FIVE ◪ ◪ ◪

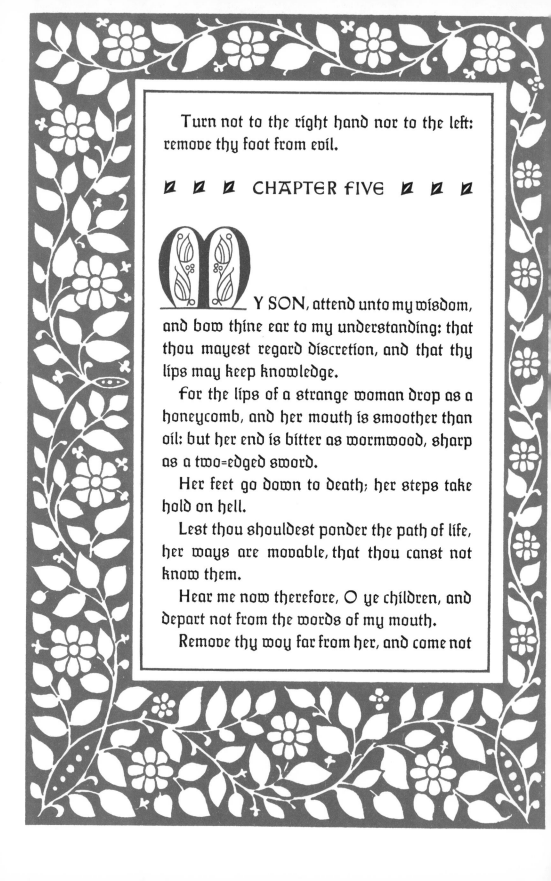

MY SON, attend unto my wisdom, and bow thine ear to my understanding: that thou mayest regard discretion, and that thy lips may keep knowledge.

For the lips of a strange woman drop as a honeycomb, and her mouth is smoother than oil: but her end is bitter as wormwood, sharp as a two=edged sword.

Her feet go down to death; her steps take hold on hell.

Lest thou shouldest ponder the path of life, her ways are movable, that thou canst not know them.

Hear me now therefore, O ye children, and depart not from the words of my mouth.

Remove thy way far from her, and come not

nigh the door of her house: lest thou give thine honor unto others, and thy years unto the cruel: lest strangers be filled with thy wealth; and thy labors be in the house of a stranger; and thou mourn at the last, when thy flesh and thy body are consumed, and say, How have I hated instruction, and my heart despised reproof; and have not obeyed the voice of my teachers, nor inclined mine ear to them that instructed me!

I was almost in all evil in the midst of the congregation and assembly.

Drink waters out of thine own cistern, and running waters out of thine own well.

Let thy fountains be dispersed abroad, and rivers of waters in the streets.

Let them be only thine own, and not stran=gers' with thee.

Let thy fountain be blessed: and rejoice with the wife of thy youth.

Let her be as the loving hind and pleasant roe; let her breasts satisfy thee at all times; and be thou ravished always with her love.

And why wilt thou, my son, be ravished

with a strange woman, and embrace the bosom of a stranger?

For the ways of man are before the eyes of the Lord, and he pondereth all his goings.

His own iniquities shall take the wicked himself, and he shall be holden with the cords of his sins.

He shall die without instruction; and in the greatness of his folly he shall go astray.

CHAPTER SIX

MY SON, if thou be surety for thy friend, if thou hast stricken thy hand with a stranger, thou art snared with the words of thy mouth, thou art taken with the words of thy mouth.

Do this now, my son, and deliver thyself, when thou art come into the hand of thy friend; go, humble thyself, and make sure thy friend.

Give not sleep to thine eyes, nor slumber to thine eyelids.

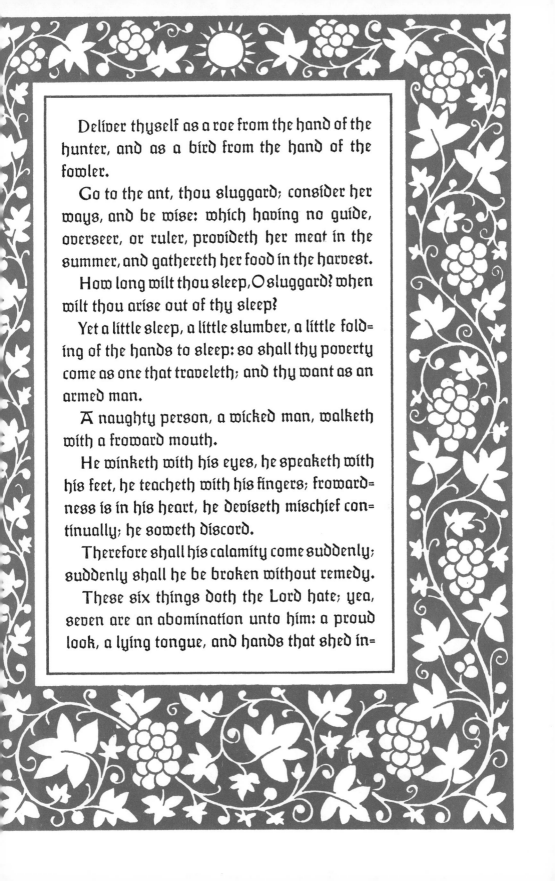

Deliver thyself as a roe from the hand of the hunter, and as a bird from the hand of the fowler.

Go to the ant, thou sluggard; consider her ways, and be wise: which having no guide, overseer, or ruler, provideth her meat in the summer, and gathereth her food in the harvest.

How long wilt thou sleep, O sluggard? when wilt thou arise out of thy sleep?

Yet a little sleep, a little slumber, a little fold= ing of the hands to sleep: so shall thy poverty come as one that traveleth; and thy want as an armed man.

A naughty person, a wicked man, walketh with a froward mouth.

He winketh with his eyes, he speaketh with his feet, he teacheth with his fingers; froward= ness is in his heart, he deviseth mischief con= tinually; he soweth discord.

Therefore shall his calamity come suddenly; suddenly shall he be broken without remedy.

These six things doth the Lord hate; yea, seven are an abomination unto him: a proud look, a lying tongue, and hands that shed in=

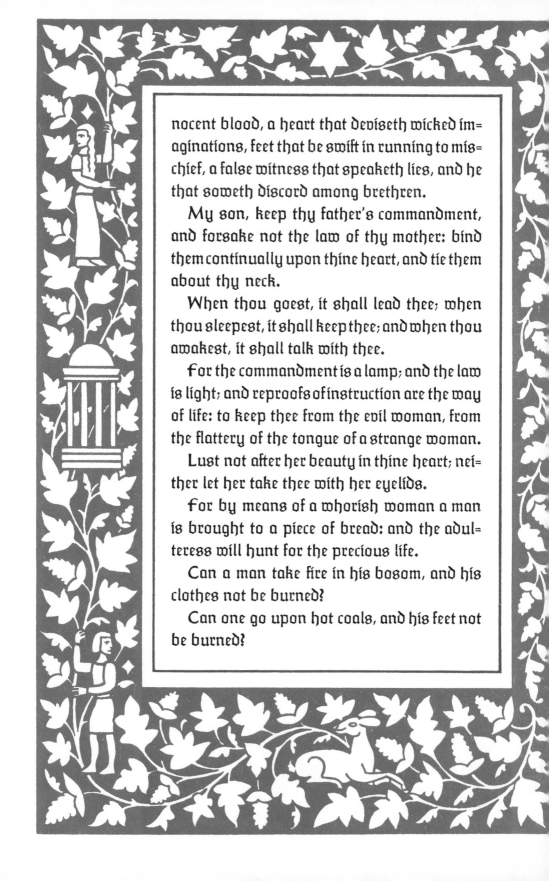

nocent blood, a heart that deviseth wicked im=
aginations, feet that be swift in running to mis=
chief, a false witness that speaketh lies, and he
that soweth discord among brethren.

My son, keep thy father's commandment,
and forsake not the law of thy mother: bind
them continually upon thine heart, and tie them
about thy neck.

When thou goest, it shall lead thee; when
thou sleepest, it shall keep thee; and when thou
awakest, it shall talk with thee.

For the commandment is a lamp; and the law
is light; and reproofs of instruction are the way
of life: to keep thee from the evil woman, from
the flattery of the tongue of a strange woman.

Lust not after her beauty in thine heart; nei=
ther let her take thee with her eyelids.

For by means of a whorish woman a man
is brought to a piece of bread: and the adul=
teress will hunt for the precious life.

Can a man take fire in his bosom, and his
clothes not be burned?

Can one go upon hot coals, and his feet not
be burned?

So he that goeth in to his neighbor's wife; whosoever toucheth her shall not be innocent.

Men do not despise a thief, if he steal to satisfy his soul when he is hungry; but if he be found, he shall restore sevenfold; he shall give all the substance of his house.

But whoso committeth adultery with a wom=an lacketh understanding: he that doeth it de=stroyeth his own soul.

A wound and dishonor shall he get; and his reproach shall not be wiped away.

For jealousy is the rage of a man: therefore he will not spare in the day of vengeance.

He will not regard any ransom; neither will he rest content, though thou givest many gifts.

▨ ▨ ▨ CHAPTER SEVEN ▨ ▨ ▨

MY SON, keep my words, and lay up my commandments with thee.

Keep my commandments, and live; and my law as the apple of thine eye.

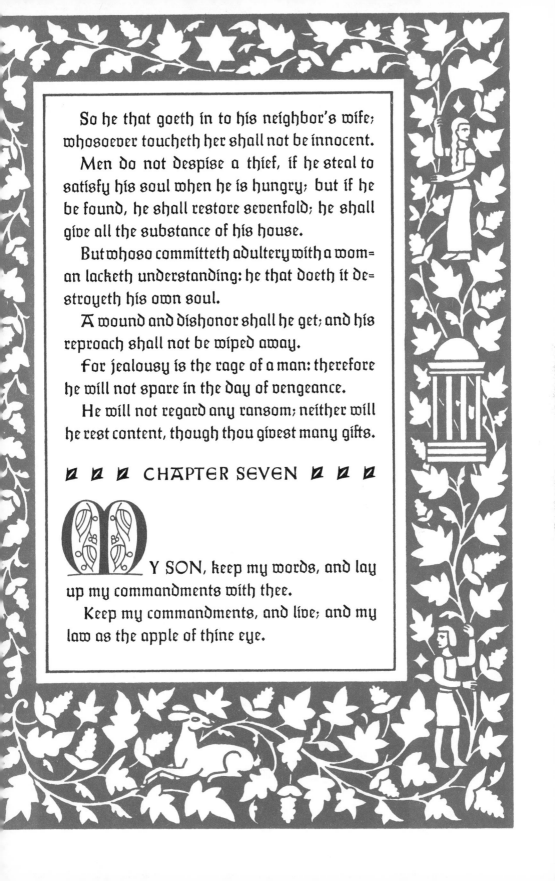

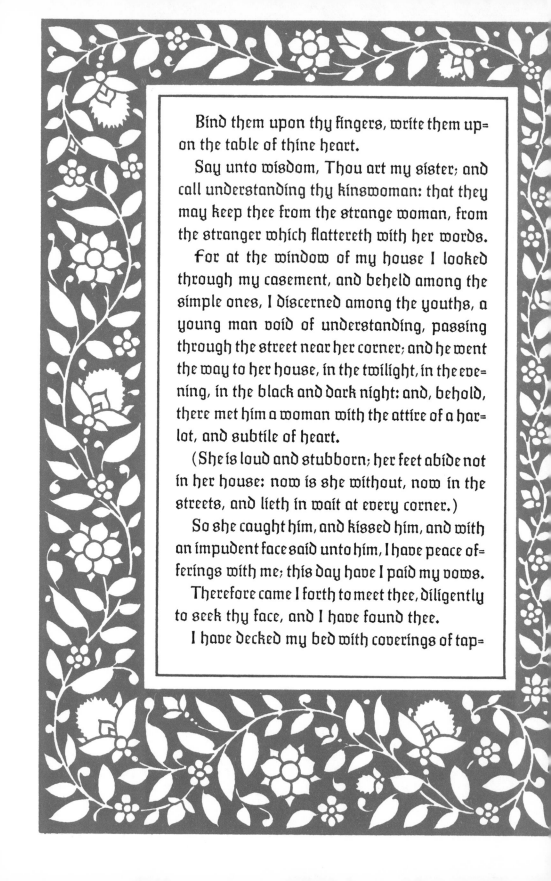

Bind them upon thy fingers, write them up=
on the table of thine heart.

Say unto wisdom, Thou art my sister; and
call understanding thy kinswoman: that they
may keep thee from the strange woman, from
the stranger which flattereth with her words.

For at the window of my house I looked
through my casement, and beheld among the
simple ones, I discerned among the youths, a
young man void of understanding, passing
through the street near her corner; and he went
the way to her house, in the twilight, in the eve=
ning, in the black and dark night: and, behold,
there met him a woman with the attire of a har=
lot, and subtile of heart.

(She is loud and stubborn; her feet abide not
in her house: now is she without, now in the
streets, and lieth in wait at every corner.)

So she caught him, and kissed him, and with
an impudent face said unto him, I have peace of=
ferings with me; this day have I paid my vows.

Therefore came I forth to meet thee, diligently
to seek thy face, and I have found thee.

I have decked my bed with coverings of tap=

estry, with carved works, with fine linen of Egypt.

I have perfumed my bed with myrrh, aloes, and cinnamon.

Come, let us take our fill of love until the morning: let us solace ourselves with loves.

For the goodman is not at home, he is gone a long journey: he hath taken a bag of money with him, and will come home at the day appointed.

With her much fair speech she caused him to yield, with the flattering of her lips she forced him.

He goeth after her straightway, as an ox goeth to the slaughter, or as a fool to the correction of the stocks; till a dart strike through his liver; as a bird hasteth to the snare, and knoweth not that it is for his life.

Hearken unto me now, therefore, O ye children, and attend to the words of my mouth.

Let not thine heart decline to her ways, go not astray in her paths.

For she hath cast down many wounded: yea, many strong men have been slain by her.

Her house is the way to hell, going down to the chambers of death.

◢ ◢ ◢ CHAPTER EIGHT ◢ ◢ ◢

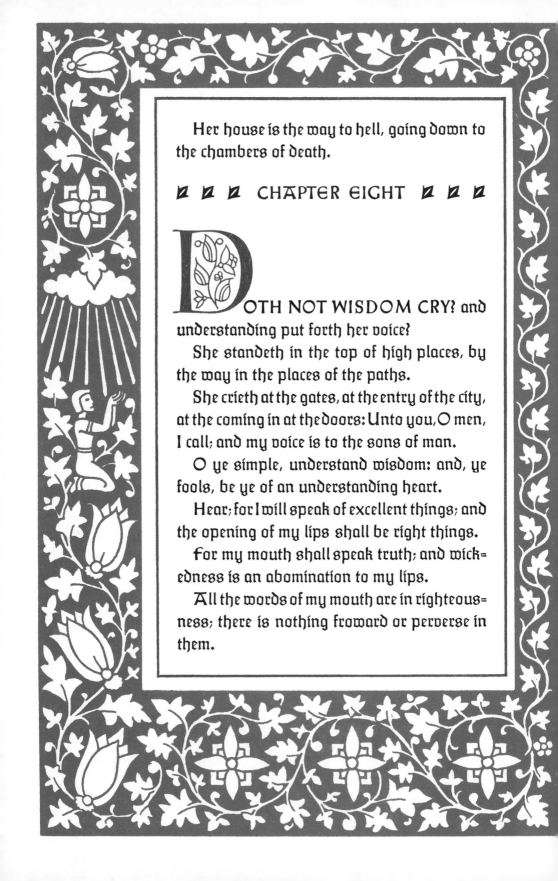

DOTH NOT WISDOM CRY? and understanding put forth her voice?

She standeth in the top of high places, by the way in the places of the paths.

She crieth at the gates, at the entry of the city, at the coming in at the doors: Unto you, O men, I call; and my voice is to the sons of man.

O ye simple, understand wisdom: and, ye fools, be ye of an understanding heart.

Hear; for I will speak of excellent things; and the opening of my lips shall be right things.

For my mouth shall speak truth; and wick= edness is an abomination to my lips.

All the words of my mouth are in righteous= ness; there is nothing froward or perverse in them.

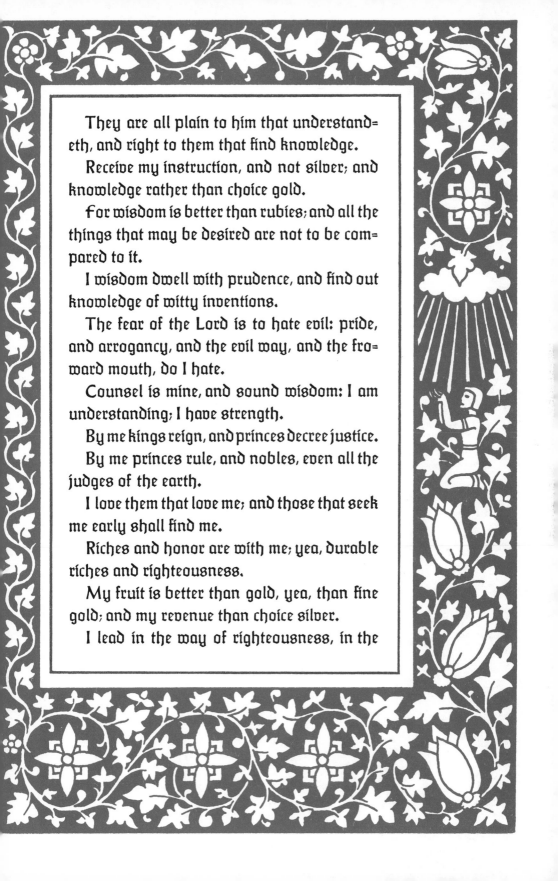

They are all plain to him that understand=
eth, and right to them that find knowledge.

Receive my instruction, and not silver; and
knowledge rather than choice gold.

For wisdom is better than rubies; and all the
things that may be desired are not to be com=
pared to it.

I wisdom dwell with prudence, and find out
knowledge of witty inventions.

The fear of the Lord is to hate evil: pride,
and arrogancy, and the evil way, and the fro=
ward mouth, do I hate.

Counsel is mine, and sound wisdom: I am
understanding; I have strength.

By me kings reign, and princes decree justice.

By me princes rule, and nobles, even all the
judges of the earth.

I love them that love me; and those that seek
me early shall find me.

Riches and honor are with me; yea, durable
riches and righteousness.

My fruit is better than gold, yea, than fine
gold; and my revenue than choice silver.

I lead in the way of righteousness, in the

midst of the paths of judgment: that I may cause those that love me to inherit substance; and I will fill their treasures.

The Lord possessed me in the beginning of his way, before his works of old.

I was set up from everlasting, from the beginning, or ever the earth was.

When there were no depths, I was brought forth; when there were no fountains abounding with water.

Before the mountains were settled, before the hills was I brought forth: while as yet he had not made the earth, nor the fields, nor the highest part of the dust of the world.

When he prepared the heavens, I was there: when he set a compass upon the face of the depth: when he established the clouds above: when he strengthened the fountains of the deep: when he gave to the sea his decree, that the waters should not pass his commandment: when he appointed the foundations of the earth: then I was by him, as one brought up with him: and I was daily his delight, rejoicing always before him; rejoicing in the habitable part of his earth; and my delights were with the sons of men.

Now therefore hearken unto me, O ye children: for blessed are they that keep my ways.

Hear instruction, and be wise, and refuse it not.

Blessed is the man that heareth me, watching daily at my gates, waiting at the posts of my doors.

For whoso findeth me findeth life, and shall obtain favor of the Lord.

But he that sinneth against me wrongeth his own soul: all they that hate me love death.

◪ ◪ ◪ CHAPTER NINE ◪ ◪ ◪

WISDOM hath builded her house, she hath hewn out her seven pillars: she hath killed her beasts; she hath mingled her wine; she hath also furnished her table.

She hath sent forth her maidens: she crieth upon the highest places of the city, Whoso is

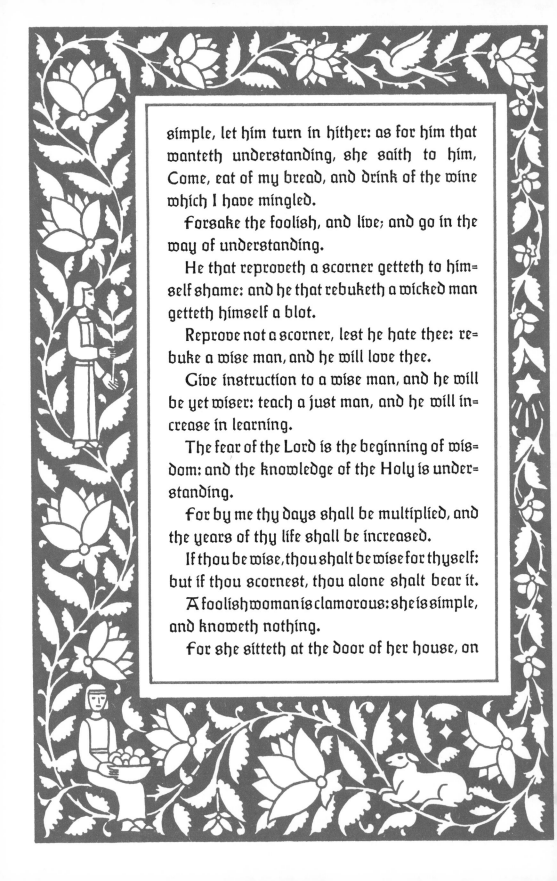

simple, let him turn in hither: as for him that wanteth understanding, she saith to him, Come, eat of my bread, and drink of the wine which I have mingled.

Forsake the foolish, and live; and go in the way of understanding.

He that reproveth a scorner getteth to him= self shame: and he that rebuketh a wicked man getteth himself a blot.

Reprove not a scorner, lest he hate thee: re= buke a wise man, and he will love thee.

Give instruction to a wise man, and he will be yet wiser: teach a just man, and he will in= crease in learning.

The fear of the Lord is the beginning of wis= dom: and the knowledge of the Holy is under= standing.

For by me thy days shall be multiplied, and the years of thy life shall be increased.

If thou be wise, thou shalt be wise for thyself: but if thou scornest, thou alone shalt bear it.

A foolish woman is clamorous: she is simple, and knoweth nothing.

For she sitteth at the door of her house, on

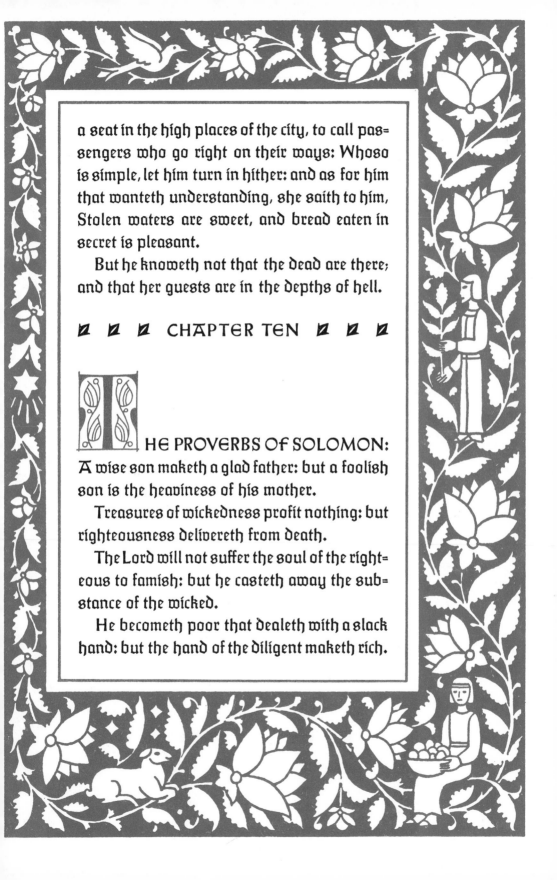

a seat in the high places of the city, to call pas=
sengers who go right on their ways: Whoso
is simple, let him turn in hither: and as for him
that wanteth understanding, she saith to him,
Stolen waters are sweet, and bread eaten in
secret is pleasant.

But he knoweth not that the dead are there;
and that her guests are in the depths of hell.

✠ ✠ ✠ CHAPTER TEN ✠ ✠ ✠

THE PROVERBS OF SOLOMON:
A wise son maketh a glad father: but a foolish
son is the heaviness of his mother.

Treasures of wickedness profit nothing: but
righteousness delivereth from death.

The Lord will not suffer the soul of the right=
eous to famish: but he casteth away the sub=
stance of the wicked.

He becometh poor that dealeth with a slack
hand: but the hand of the diligent maketh rich.

He that gathereth in summer is a wise son: but he that sleepeth in harvest is a son that causeth shame.

Blessings are upon the head of the just: but violence covereth the mouth of the wicked.

The memory of the just is blessed: but the name of the wicked shall rot.

The wise in heart will receive command=ments: but a prating fool shall fall.

He that walketh uprightly walketh surely: but he that perverteth his ways shall be known.

He that winketh with the eye causeth sorrow: but a prating fool shall fall.

The mouth of a righteous man is a well of life: but violence covereth the mouth of the wicked.

Hatred stirreth up strifes: but love covereth all sins.

In the lips of him that hath understanding wisdom is found: but a rod is for the back of him that is void of understanding.

Wise men lay up knowledge: but the mouth of the foolish is near destruction.

The rich man's wealth is his strong city:

the destruction of the poor is their poverty.

The labor of the righteous tendeth to life: the fruit of the wicked to sin.

He is in the way of life that keepeth instruc= tion: but he that refuseth reproof erreth.

He that hideth hatred with lying lips, and he that uttereth a slander, is a fool.

In the multitude of words there wanteth not sin: but he that refraineth his lips is wise.

The tongue of the just is as choice silver: the heart of the wicked is little worth.

The lips of the righteous feed many: but fools die for want of wisdom.

The blessing of the Lord, it maketh rich, and he addeth no sorrow with it.

It is as sport to a fool to do mischief: but a man of understanding hath wisdom.

The fear of the wicked, it shall come upon him: but the desire of the righteous shall be granted.

As the whirlwind passeth, so is the wicked no more: but the righteous is an everlasting foundation.

As vinegar to the teeth, and as smoke to the eyes, so is the sluggard to them that send him.

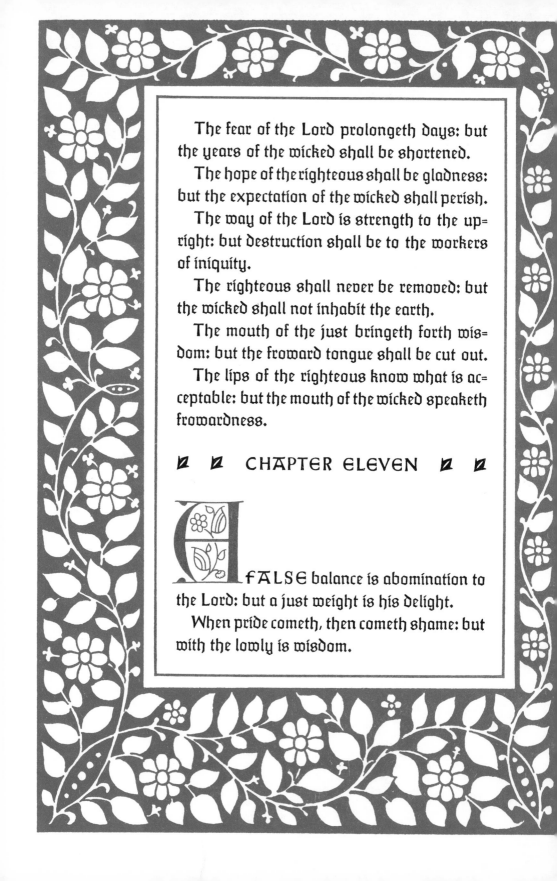

The fear of the Lord prolongeth days: but the years of the wicked shall be shortened.

The hope of the righteous shall be gladness: but the expectation of the wicked shall perish.

The way of the Lord is strength to the upright: but destruction shall be to the workers of iniquity.

The righteous shall never be removed: but the wicked shall not inhabit the earth.

The mouth of the just bringeth forth wisdom: but the froward tongue shall be cut out.

The lips of the righteous know what is acceptable: but the mouth of the wicked speaketh frowardness.

CHAPTER ELEVEN

A FALSE balance is abomination to the Lord: but a just weight is his delight.

When pride cometh, then cometh shame: but with the lowly is wisdom.

The integrity of the upright shall guide them: but the perverseness of transgressors shall destroy them.

Riches profit not in the day of wrath: but righteousness delivereth from death.

The righteousness of the perfect shall direct his way: but the wicked shall fall by his own wickedness.

The righteousness of the upright shall deliver them: but transgressors shall be taken in their own naughtiness.

When a wicked man dieth, his expectation shall perish: and the hope of unjust men perisheth.

The righteous is delivered out of trouble, and the wicked cometh in his stead.

A hypocrite with his mouth destroyeth his neighbor: but through knowledge shall the just be delivered.

When it goeth well with the righteous, the city rejoiceth: and when the wicked perish, there is shouting.

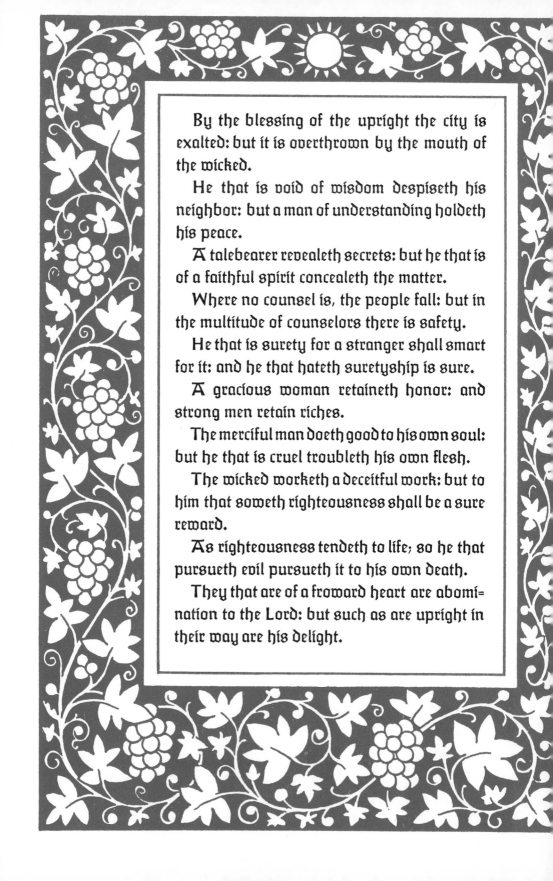

By the blessing of the upright the city is exalted: but it is overthrown by the mouth of the wicked.

He that is void of wisdom despiseth his neighbor: but a man of understanding holdeth his peace.

A talebearer revealeth secrets: but he that is of a faithful spirit concealeth the matter.

Where no counsel is, the people fall: but in the multitude of counselors there is safety.

He that is surety for a stranger shall smart for it: and he that hateth suretyship is sure.

A gracious woman retaineth honor: and strong men retain riches.

The merciful man doeth good to his own soul: but he that is cruel troubleth his own flesh.

The wicked worketh a deceitful work: but to him that soweth righteousness shall be a sure reward.

As righteousness tendeth to life; so he that pursueth evil pursueth it to his own death.

They that are of a froward heart are abomi= nation to the Lord: but such as are upright in their way are his delight.

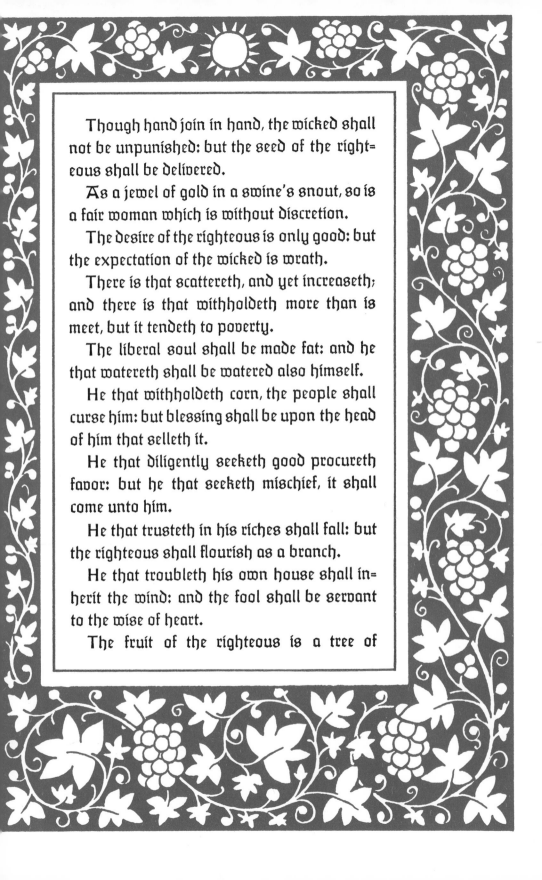

Though hand join in hand, the wicked shall not be unpunished: but the seed of the right= eous shall be delivered.

As a jewel of gold in a swine's snout, so is a fair woman which is without discretion.

The desire of the righteous is only good: but the expectation of the wicked is wrath.

There is that scattereth, and yet increaseth; and there is that withholdeth more than is meet, but it tendeth to poverty.

The liberal soul shall be made fat: and he that watereth shall be watered also himself.

He that withholdeth corn, the people shall curse him: but blessing shall be upon the head of him that selleth it.

He that diligently seeketh good procureth favor: but he that seeketh mischief, it shall come unto him.

He that trusteth in his riches shall fall: but the righteous shall flourish as a branch.

He that troubleth his own house shall in= herit the wind: and the fool shall be servant to the wise of heart.

The fruit of the righteous is a tree of

life; and he that winneth souls is wise.

Behold, the righteous shall be recompensed in the earth: much more the wicked and the sinner.

▨ ▨ CHAPTER TWELVE ▨ ▨

WHOSO loveth instruction loveth knowledge: but he that hateth reproof is brutish.

A good man obtaineth favor of the Lord: but a man of wicked devices will he condemn.

A man shall not be established by wicked= ness: but the root of the righteous shall not be moved.

A virtuous woman is a crown to her hus= band: but she that maketh ashamed is as rot= tenness in his bones.

The thoughts of the righteous are right: but the counsels of the wicked are deceit.

The words of the wicked are to lie in wait for blood: but the mouth of the upright shall de= liver them.

The wicked are overthrown, and are not: but the house of the righteous shall stand.

A man shall be commended according to his wisdom: but he that is of a perverse heart shall be despised.

He that is despised, and hath a servant, is better than he that honoreth himself, and lack=eth bread.

A righteous man regardeth the life of his beast: but the tender mercies of the wicked are cruel.

He that tilleth his land shall be satisfied with bread: but he that followeth vain persons is void of understanding.

The wicked desireth the net of evil men: but the root of the righteous yieldeth fruit.

The wicked is snared by the transgression of his lips: but the just shall come out of trouble.

A man shall be satisfied with good by the fruit of his mouth: and the recompense of a man's hands shall be rendered unto him.

The way of a fool is right in his own eyes: but he that hearkeneth unto counsel is wise.

A fool's wrath is presently known: but a
prudent man covereth shame.

He that speaketh truth showeth forth right=
eousness: but a false witness deceit.

There is that speaketh like the piercings of a
sword: but the tongue of the wise is health.

The lip of truth shall be established for ever:
but a lying tongue is but for a moment.

Deceit is in the heart of them that imagine
evil: but to the counselors of peace is joy.

There shall no evil happen to the just: but
the wicked shall be filled with mischief.

Lying lips are abomination to the Lord: but
they that deal truly are his delight.

A prudent man concealeth knowledge: but
the heart of fools proclaimeth foolishness.

The hand of the diligent shall bear rule:
but the slothful shall be under tribute.

Heaviness in the heart of man maketh it
stoop: but a good word maketh it glad.

The righteous is more excellent than his
neighbor: but the way of the wicked seduceth
them.

The slothful man roasteth not that which

he took in hunting: but the substance of a diligent man is precious.

In the way of righteousness is life; and in the pathway thereof there is no death.

⬧ ⬧ CHAPTER THIRTEEN ⬧ ⬧

A WISE SON heareth his father's instruction: but a scorner heareth not rebuke.

A man shall eat good by the fruit of his mouth: but the soul of the transgressors shall eat violence.

He that keepeth his mouth keepeth his life: but he that openeth wide his lips shall have destruction.

The soul of the sluggard desireth, and hath nothing: but the soul of the diligent shall be made fat.

A righteous man hateth lying: but a wicked man is loathsome, and cometh to shame.

Righteousness keepeth him that is upright

in the way: but wickedness overthroweth the sinner.

There is that maketh himself rich, yet hath nothing: there is that maketh himself poor, yet hath great riches.

The ransom of a man's life are his riches: but the poor heareth not rebuke.

The light of the righteous rejoiceth: but the lamp of the wicked shall be put out.

Only by pride cometh contention: but with the well advised is wisdom.

Wealth gotten by vanity shall be diminished: but he that gathereth by labor shall increase.

Hope deferred maketh the heart sick: but when the desire cometh, it is a tree of life.

Whoso despiseth the word shall be de=stroyed: but he that feareth the commandment shall be rewarded.

The law of the wise is a fountain of life, to depart from the snares of death.

Good understanding giveth favor: but the way of transgressors is hard.

Every prudent man dealeth with knowl=edge: but a fool layeth open his folly.

A wicked messenger falleth into mischief: but a faithful ambassador is health.

Poverty and shame shall be to him that refuseth instruction: but he that regardeth reproof shall be honored.

The desire accomplished is sweet to the soul: but it is abomination to fools to depart from evil.

He that walketh with wise men shall be wise: but a companion of fools shall be destroyed.

Evil pursueth sinners: but to the righteous good shall be repaid.

A good man leaveth an inheritance to his children's children: and the wealth of the sin=ner is laid up for the just.

Much food is in the tillage of the poor: but there is that is destroyed for want of judgment.

He that spareth his rod hateth his son: but he that loveth him chasteneth him betimes.

The righteous eateth to the satisfying of his soul: but the belly of the wicked shall want.

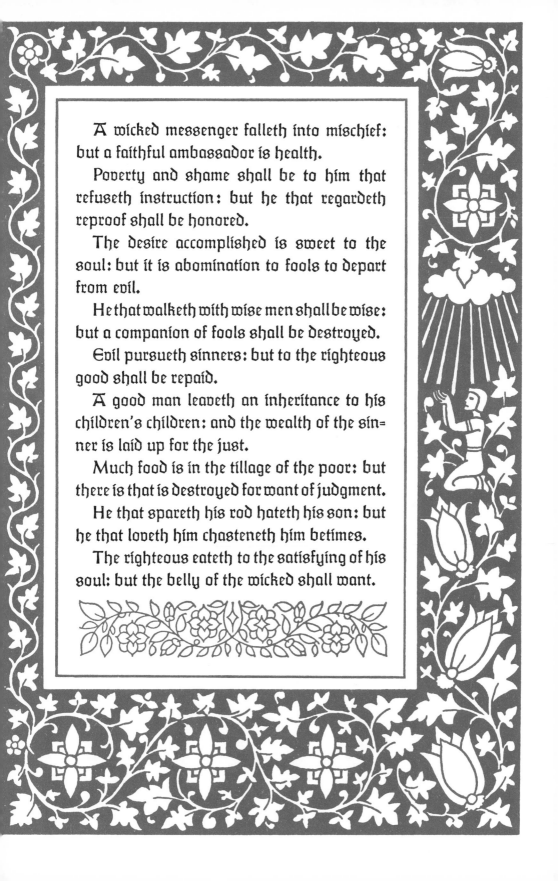

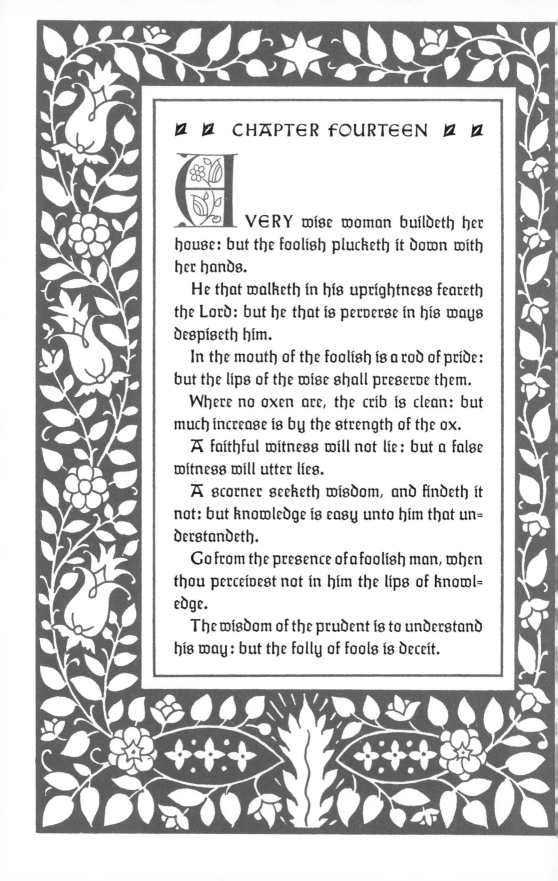

◪ ◪ CHAPTER FOURTEEN ◪ ◪

VERY wise woman buildeth her house: but the foolish plucketh it down with her hands.

He that walketh in his uprightness feareth the Lord: but he that is perverse in his ways despiseth him.

In the mouth of the foolish is a rod of pride: but the lips of the wise shall preserve them.

Where no oxen are, the crib is clean: but much increase is by the strength of the ox.

A faithful witness will not lie: but a false witness will utter lies.

A scorner seeketh wisdom, and findeth it not: but knowledge is easy unto him that understandeth.

Go from the presence of a foolish man, when thou perceivest not in him the lips of knowledge.

The wisdom of the prudent is to understand his way: but the folly of fools is deceit.

Fools make a mock at sin: but among the righteous there is favor.

The heart knoweth his own bitterness; and a stranger doth not intermeddle with his joy.

The house of the wicked shall be over=thrown: but the tabernacle of the upright shall flourish.

There is a way which seemeth right unto a man; but the end thereof are the ways of death.

Even in laughter the heart is sorrowful; and the end of that mirth is heaviness.

The backslider in heart shall be filled with his own ways: and a good man shall be satis=fied from himself.

The simple believeth every word: but the prudent man looketh well to his going.

A wise man feareth, and departeth from evil: but the fool rageth, and is confident.

He that is soon angry dealeth foolishly: and a man of wicked devices is hated.

The simple inherit folly: but the prudent are crowned with knowledge.

The evil bow before the good; and the wick=ed at the gates of the righteous.

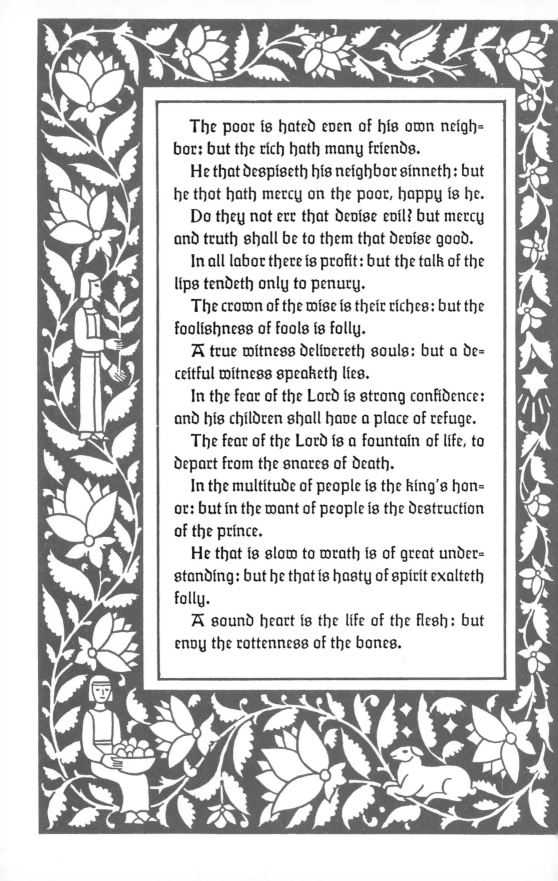

The poor is hated even of his own neigh=bor: but the rich hath many friends.

He that despiseth his neighbor sinneth: but he that hath mercy on the poor, happy is he.

Do they not err that devise evil? but mercy and truth shall be to them that devise good.

In all labor there is profit: but the talk of the lips tendeth only to penury.

The crown of the wise is their riches: but the foolishness of fools is folly.

A true witness delivereth souls: but a de=ceitful witness speaketh lies.

In the fear of the Lord is strong confidence: and his children shall have a place of refuge.

The fear of the Lord is a fountain of life, to depart from the snares of death.

In the multitude of people is the king's hon=or: but in the want of people is the destruction of the prince.

He that is slow to wrath is of great under=standing: but he that is hasty of spirit exalteth folly.

A sound heart is the life of the flesh: but envy the rottenness of the bones.

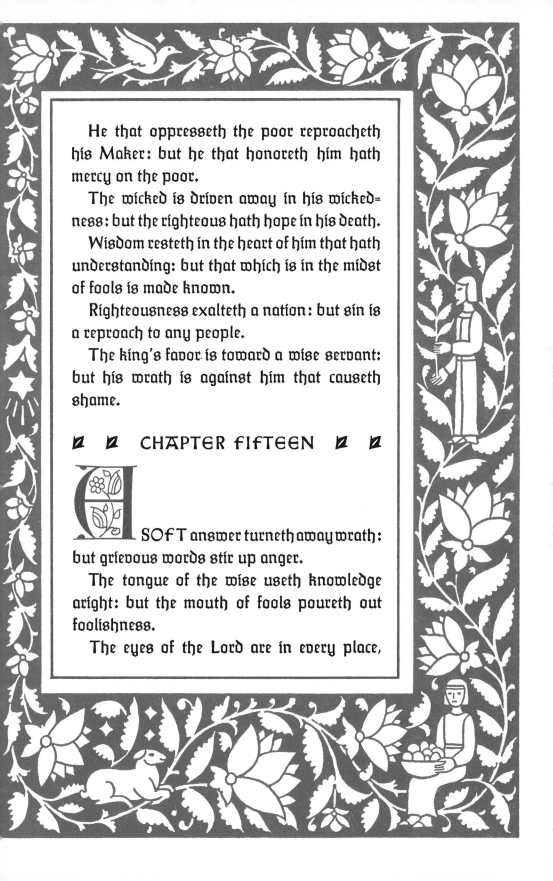

He that oppresseth the poor reproacheth his Maker: but he that honoreth him hath mercy on the poor.

The wicked is driven away in his wicked= ness: but the righteous hath hope in his death.

Wisdom resteth in the heart of him that hath understanding: but that which is in the midst of fools is made known.

Righteousness exalteth a nation: but sin is a reproach to any people.

The king's favor is toward a wise servant: but his wrath is against him that causeth shame.

CHAPTER FIFTEEN

A SOFT answer turneth away wrath: but grievous words stir up anger.

The tongue of the wise useth knowledge aright: but the mouth of fools poureth out foolishness.

The eyes of the Lord are in every place,

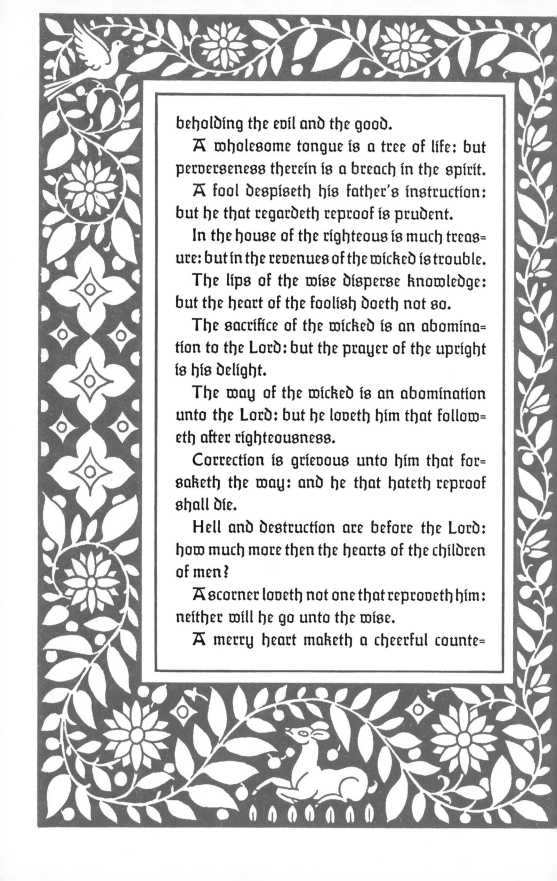

beholding the evil and the good.

A wholesome tongue is a tree of life: but perverseness therein is a breach in the spirit.

A fool despiseth his father's instruction: but he that regardeth reproof is prudent.

In the house of the righteous is much treas=ure: but in the revenues of the wicked is trouble.

The lips of the wise disperse knowledge: but the heart of the foolish doeth not so.

The sacrifice of the wicked is an abomina=tion to the Lord: but the prayer of the upright is his delight.

The way of the wicked is an abomination unto the Lord: but he loveth him that follow=eth after righteousness.

Correction is grievous unto him that for=saketh the way: and he that hateth reproof shall die.

Hell and destruction are before the Lord: how much more then the hearts of the children of men?

A scorner loveth not one that reproveth him: neither will he go unto the wise.

A merry heart maketh a cheerful counte=

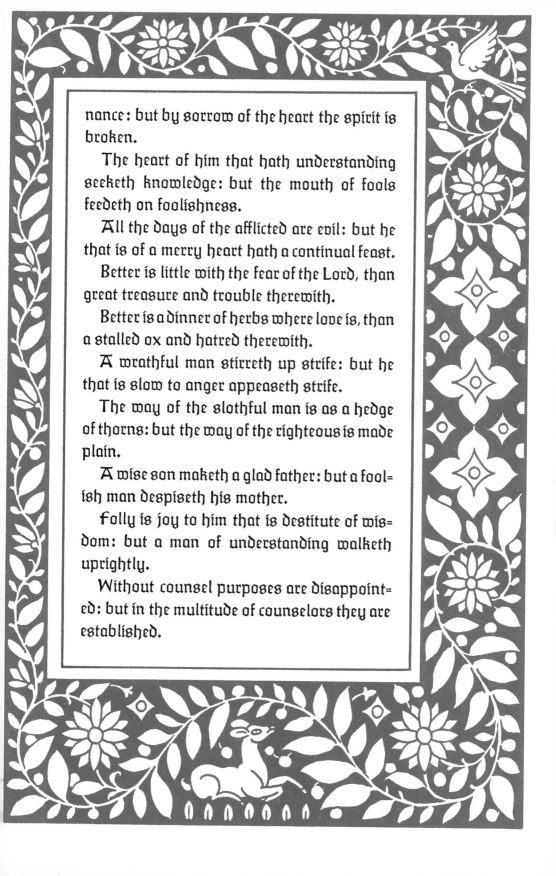

nance: but by sorrow of the heart the spirit is broken.

The heart of him that hath understanding seeketh knowledge: but the mouth of fools feedeth on foolishness.

All the days of the afflicted are evil: but he that is of a merry heart hath a continual feast.

Better is little with the fear of the Lord, than great treasure and trouble therewith.

Better is a dinner of herbs where love is, than a stalled ox and hatred therewith.

A wrathful man stirreth up strife: but he that is slow to anger appeaseth strife.

The way of the slothful man is as a hedge of thorns: but the way of the righteous is made plain.

A wise son maketh a glad father: but a foolish man despiseth his mother.

Folly is joy to him that is destitute of wisdom: but a man of understanding walketh uprightly.

Without counsel purposes are disappointed: but in the multitude of counselors they are established.

A man hath joy by the answer of his mouth: and a word spoken in due season, how good is it!

The way of life is above to the wise, that he may depart from hell beneath.

The Lord will destroy the house of the proud: but he will establish the border of the widow.

The thoughts of the wicked are an abomination to the Lord: but the words of the pure are pleasant words.

He that is greedy of gain troubleth his own house; but he that hateth gifts shall live.

The heart of the righteous studieth to answer: but the mouth of the wicked poureth out evil things.

The Lord is far from the wicked: but he heareth the prayer of the righteous.

The light of the eyes rejoiceth the heart: and a good report maketh the bones fat.

The ear that heareth the reproof of life abideth among the wise.

He that refuseth instruction despiseth his own soul: but he that heareth reproof getteth understanding.

The fear of the Lord is the instruction of wisdom; and before honor is humility.

✠ ✠ CHAPTER SIXTEEN ✠ ✠

THE preparations of the heart in man, and the answer of the tongue, is from the Lord.

All the ways of a man are clean in his own eyes; but the Lord weigheth the spirits.

Commit thy works unto the Lord, and thy thoughts shall be established.

The Lord hath made all things for himself: yea, even the wicked for the day of evil.

Every one that is proud in heart is an abom= ination to the Lord: though hand join in hand, he shall not be unpunished.

By mercy and truth iniquity is purged: and by the fear of the Lord men depart from evil.

When a man's ways please the Lord, he maketh even his enemies to be at peace with him.

Better is a little with righteousness, than great revenues without right.

A man's heart deviseth his way: but the Lord directeth his steps.

A divine sentence is in the lips of the king: his mouth transgresseth not in judgment.

A just weight and balance are the Lord's: all the weights of the bag are his work.

It is an abomination to kings to commit wickedness: for the throne is established by righteousness.

Righteous lips are the delight of kings; and they love him that speaketh right.

The wrath of a king is as messengers of death: but a wise man will pacify it.

In the light of the king's countenance is life; and his favor is as a cloud of the latter rain.

How much better is it to get wisdom than gold! and to get understanding rather to be chosen than silver!

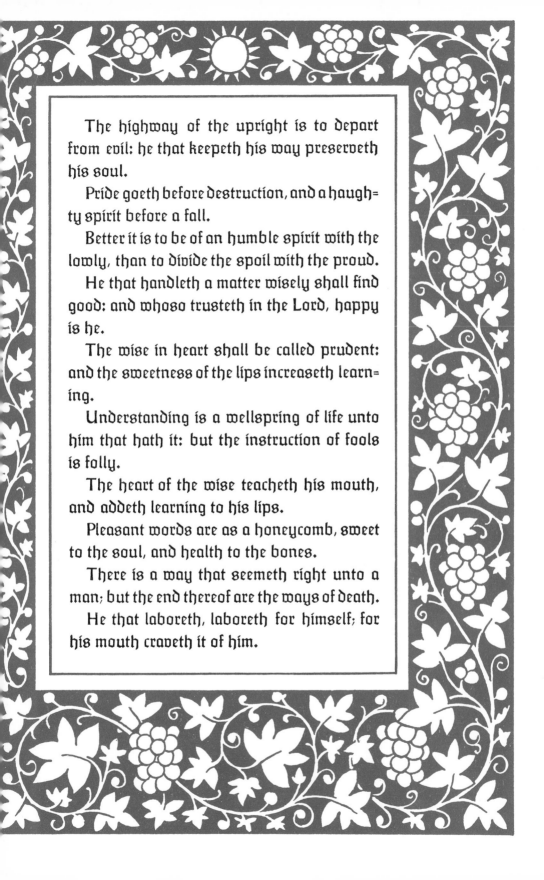

The highway of the upright is to depart from evil: he that keepeth his way preserveth his soul.

Pride goeth before destruction, and a haughty spirit before a fall.

Better it is to be of an humble spirit with the lowly, than to divide the spoil with the proud.

He that handleth a matter wisely shall find good: and whoso trusteth in the Lord, happy is he.

The wise in heart shall be called prudent: and the sweetness of the lips increaseth learning.

Understanding is a wellspring of life unto him that hath it: but the instruction of fools is folly.

The heart of the wise teacheth his mouth, and addeth learning to his lips.

Pleasant words are as a honeycomb, sweet to the soul, and health to the bones.

There is a way that seemeth right unto a man; but the end thereof are the ways of death.

He that laboreth, laboreth for himself; for his mouth craveth it of him.

An ungodly man diggeth up evil: and in his lips there is as a burning fire.

A froward man soweth strife: and a whisperer separateth chief friends.

A violent man enticeth his neighbor, and leadeth him into the way that is not good.

He shutteth his eyes to devise froward things: moving his lips he bringeth evil to pass.

The hoary head is a crown of glory, if it be found in the way of righteousness.

He that is slow to anger is better than the mighty; and he that ruleth his spirit than he that taketh a city.

The lot is cast into the lap; but the whole disposing thereof is of the Lord.

❖ ❖ CHAPTER SEVENTEEN ❖ ❖

BETTER is a dry morsel, and quietness therewith, than a house full of sacrifices with strife.

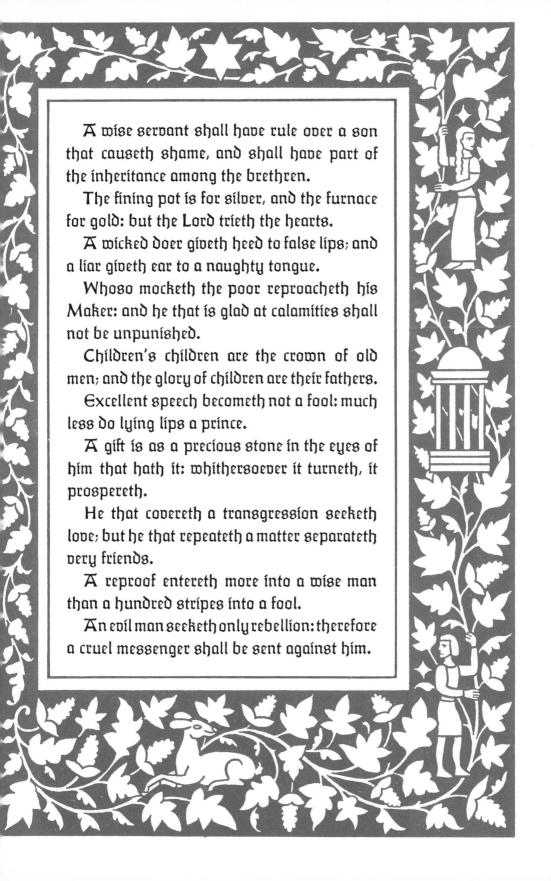

A wise servant shall have rule over a son that causeth shame, and shall have part of the inheritance among the brethren.

The fining pot is for silver, and the furnace for gold: but the Lord trieth the hearts.

A wicked doer giveth heed to false lips; and a liar giveth ear to a naughty tongue.

Whoso mocketh the poor reproacheth his Maker: and he that is glad at calamities shall not be unpunished.

Children's children are the crown of old men; and the glory of children are their fathers.

Excellent speech becometh not a fool: much less do lying lips a prince.

A gift is as a precious stone in the eyes of him that hath it: whithersoever it turneth, it prospereth.

He that covereth a transgression seeketh love; but he that repeateth a matter separateth very friends.

A reproof entereth more into a wise man than a hundred stripes into a fool.

An evil man seeketh only rebellion: therefore a cruel messenger shall be sent against him.

Let a bear robbed of her whelps meet a man, rather than a fool in his folly.

Whoso rewardeth evil for good, evil shall not depart from his house.

The beginning of strife is as when one let= teth out water: therefore leave off contention, before it be meddled with.

He that justifieth the wicked, and he that condemneth the just, even they both are abom= ination to the Lord.

Wherefore is there a price in the hand of a fool to get wisdom, seeing he hath no heart to it?

A friend loveth at all times, and a brother is born for adversity.

A man void of understanding striketh hands, and becometh surety in the presence of his friend.

He loveth transgression that loveth strife: and he that exalteth his gate seeketh destruc= tion.

He that hath a froward heart findeth no good: and he that hath a perverse tongue fall= eth into mischief.

He that begetteth a fool doeth it to his sor=

row: and the father of a fool hath no joy.

A merry heart doeth good like a medicine: but a broken spirit drieth the bones.

A wicked man taketh a gift out of the bosom to pervert the ways of judgment.

Wisdom is before him that hath understand= ing; but the eyes of a fool are in the ends of the earth.

A foolish son is a grief to his father, and bitterness to her that bare him.

Also to punish the just is not good, nor to strike princes for equity.

He that hath knowledge spareth his words: and a man of understanding is of an excellent spirit.

Even a fool, when he holdeth his peace, is counted wise: and he that shutteth his lips is esteemed a man of understanding.

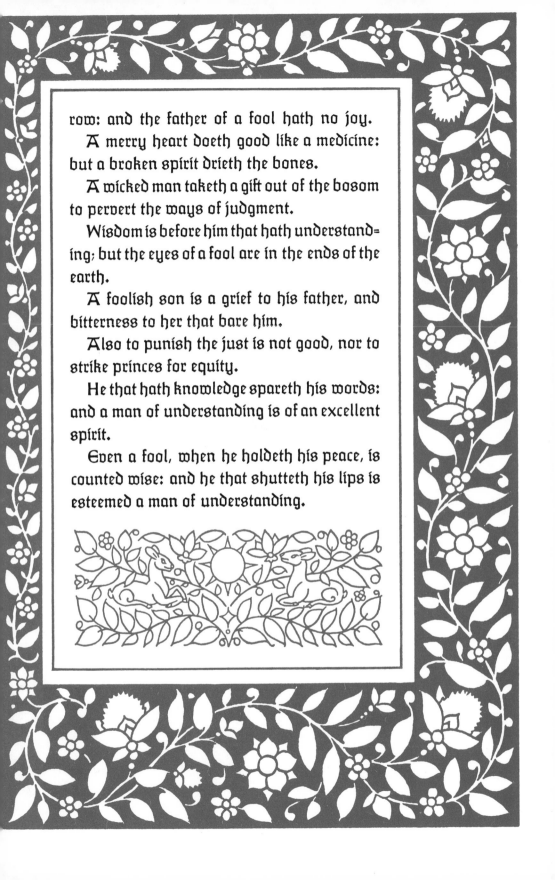

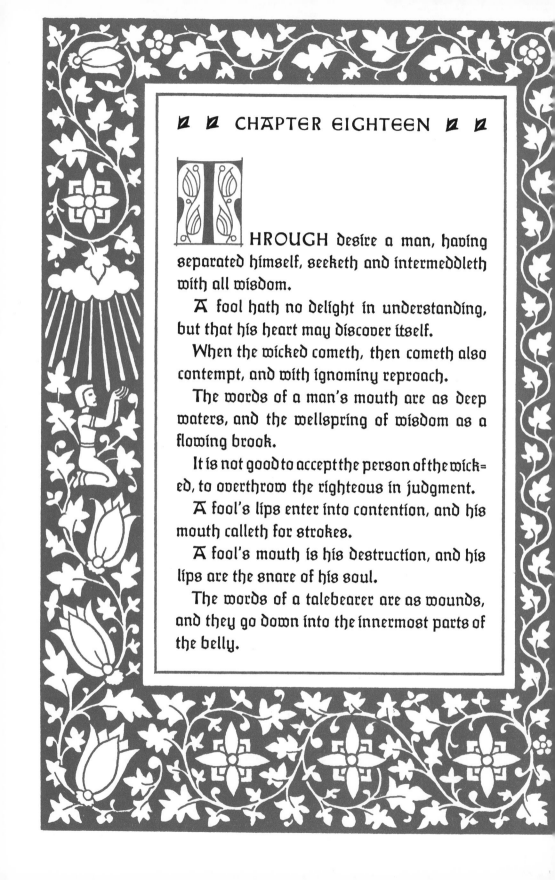

❧ ❧ CHAPTER EIGHTEEN ❧ ❧

THROUGH desire a man, having separated himself, seeketh and intermeddleth with all wisdom.

A fool hath no delight in understanding, but that his heart may discover itself.

When the wicked cometh, then cometh also contempt, and with ignominy reproach.

The words of a man's mouth are as deep waters, and the wellspring of wisdom as a flowing brook.

It is not good to accept the person of the wick= ed, to overthrow the righteous in judgment.

A fool's lips enter into contention, and his mouth calleth for strokes.

A fool's mouth is his destruction, and his lips are the snare of his soul.

The words of a talebearer are as wounds, and they go down into the innermost parts of the belly.

He also that is slothful in his work is broth= er to him that is a great waster.

The name of the Lord is a strong tower: the righteous runneth into it, and is safe.

The rich man's wealth is his strong city, and as a high wall in his own conceit.

Before destruction the heart of man is haugh= ty; and before honor is humility.

He that answereth a matter before he hear= eth it, it is folly and shame unto him.

The spirit of a man will sustain his infirmi= ty; but a wounded spirit who can bear?

The heart of the prudent getteth knowledge; and the ear of the wise seeketh knowledge.

A man's gift maketh room for him, and bringeth him before great men.

He that is first in his own cause seemeth just; but his neighbor cometh and searcheth him.

The lot causeth contentions to cease, and parteth between the mighty.

A brother offended is harder to be won than a strong city: and their contentions are like the bars of a castle.

A man's belly shall be satisfied with the fruit of his mouth; and with the increase of his lips shall he be filled.

Death and life are in the power of the tongue: and they that love it shall eat the fruit thereof.

Whoso findeth a wife findeth a good thing, and obtaineth favor of the Lord.

The poor useth entreaties; but the rich answereth roughly.

A man that hath friends must show himself friendly: and there is a friend that sticketh closer than a brother.

◆ ◆ CHAPTER NINETEEN ◆ ◆

BETTER is the poor that walketh in his integrity, than he that is perverse in his lips, and is a fool.

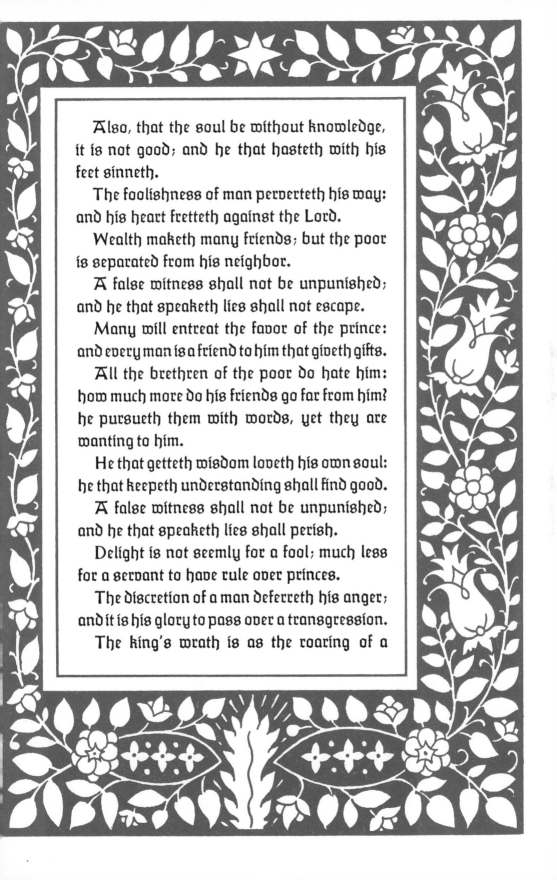

Also, that the soul be without knowledge, it is not good; and he that hasteth with his feet sinneth.

The foolishness of man perverteth his way: and his heart fretteth against the Lord.

Wealth maketh many friends; but the poor is separated from his neighbor.

A false witness shall not be unpunished; and he that speaketh lies shall not escape.

Many will entreat the favor of the prince: and every man is a friend to him that giveth gifts.

All the brethren of the poor do hate him: how much more do his friends go far from him? he pursueth them with words, yet they are wanting to him.

He that getteth wisdom loveth his own soul: he that keepeth understanding shall find good.

A false witness shall not be unpunished; and he that speaketh lies shall perish.

Delight is not seemly for a fool; much less for a servant to have rule over princes.

The discretion of a man deferreth his anger; and it is his glory to pass over a transgression.

The king's wrath is as the roaring of a

lion; but his favor is as dew upon the grass.

A foolish son is the calamity of his father: and the contentions of a wife are a continual dropping.

House and riches are the inheritance of fathers: and a prudent wife is from the Lord.

Slothfulness casteth into a deep sleep; and an idle soul shall suffer hunger.

He that keepeth the commandment keepeth his own soul; but he that despiseth his ways shall die.

He that hath pity upon the poor lendeth unto the Lord; and that which he hath given will he pay him again.

Chasten thy son while there is hope, and let not thy soul spare for his crying.

A man of great wrath shall suffer punishment: for if thou deliver him, yet thou must do it again.

Hear counsel, and receive instruction, that thou mayest be wise in thy latter end.

There are many devices in a man's heart; nevertheless the counsel of the Lord, that shall stand.

The desire of a man is his kindness: and a poor man is better than a liar.

The fear of the Lord tendeth to life: and he that hath it shall abide satisfied; he shall not be visited with evil.

A slothful man hideth his hand in his bosom, and will not so much as bring it to his mouth again.

Smite a scorner, and the simple will beware: and reprove one that hath understanding, and he will understand knowledge.

He that wasteth his father, and chaseth away his mother, is a son that causeth shame, and bringeth reproach.

Cease, my son, to hear the instruction that causeth to err from the words of knowledge.

An ungodly witness scorneth judgment: and the mouth of the wicked devoureth iniquity.

Judgments are prepared for scorners, and stripes for the back of fools.

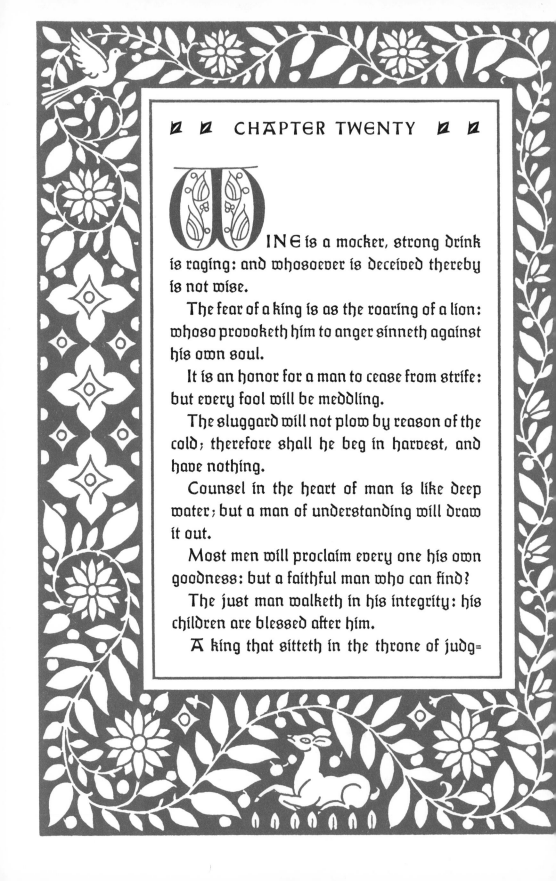

CHAPTER TWENTY

WINE is a mocker, strong drink is raging: and whosoever is deceived thereby is not wise.

The fear of a king is as the roaring of a lion: whoso provoketh him to anger sinneth against his own soul.

It is an honor for a man to cease from strife: but every fool will be meddling.

The sluggard will not plow by reason of the cold; therefore shall he beg in harvest, and have nothing.

Counsel in the heart of man is like deep water; but a man of understanding will draw it out.

Most men will proclaim every one his own goodness: but a faithful man who can find?

The just man walketh in his integrity: his children are blessed after him.

A king that sitteth in the throne of judg=

ment scattereth away all evil with his eyes.

Who can say, I have made my heart clean, I am pure from my sin?

Divers weights, and divers measures, both of them are alike abomination to the Lord.

Even a child is known by his doings, whether his work be pure, and whether it be right.

The hearing ear, and the seeing eye, the Lord hath made even both of them.

Love not sleep, lest thou come to poverty: open thine eyes, and thou shalt be satisfied with bread.

It is naught, it is naught, saith the buyer: but when he is gone his way, then he boasteth.

There is gold, and a multitude of rubies: but the lips of knowledge are a precious jewel.

Take his garment that is surety for a stranger: and take a pledge of him for a strange woman.

Bread of deceit is sweet to a man; but afterward his mouth shall be filled with gravel.

Every purpose is established by counsel: and with good advice make war.

He that goeth about as a talebearer reveal=

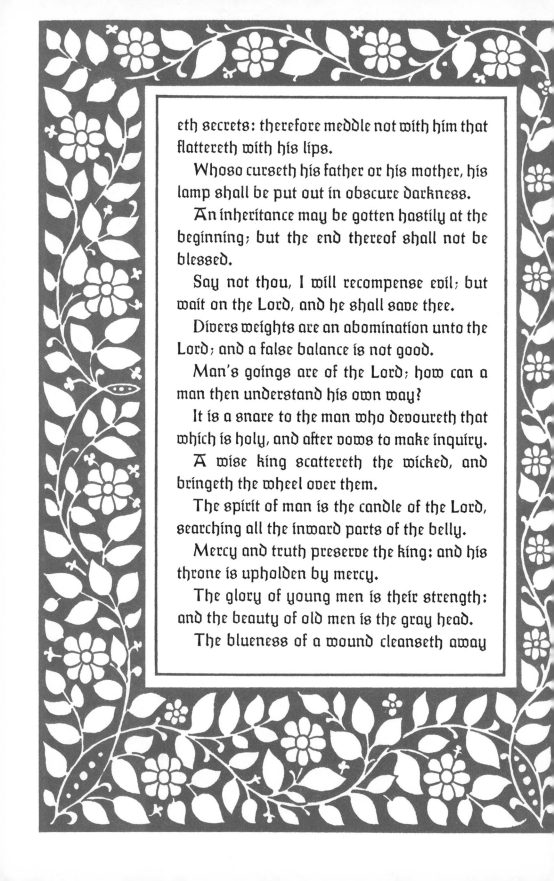

eth secrets: therefore meddle not with him that flattereth with his lips.

Whoso curseth his father or his mother, his lamp shall be put out in obscure darkness.

An inheritance may be gotten hastily at the beginning; but the end thereof shall not be blessed.

Say not thou, I will recompense evil; but wait on the Lord, and he shall save thee.

Divers weights are an abomination unto the Lord; and a false balance is not good.

Man's goings are of the Lord; how can a man then understand his own way?

It is a snare to the man who devoureth that which is holy, and after vows to make inquiry.

A wise king scattereth the wicked, and bringeth the wheel over them.

The spirit of man is the candle of the Lord, searching all the inward parts of the belly.

Mercy and truth preserve the king: and his throne is upholden by mercy.

The glory of young men is their strength: and the beauty of old men is the gray head.

The blueness of a wound cleanseth away

evil: so do stripes the inward parts of the belly.

✠ ✠ CHAPTER TWENTY=ONE ✠ ✠

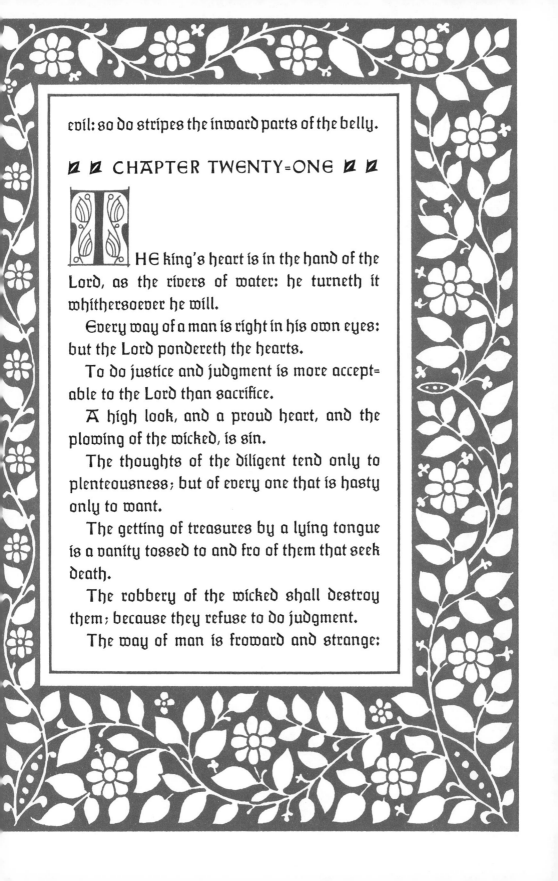

HE king's heart is in the hand of the Lord, as the rivers of water: he turneth it whithersoever he will.

Every way of a man is right in his own eyes: but the Lord pondereth the hearts.

To do justice and judgment is more accept= able to the Lord than sacrifice.

A high look, and a proud heart, and the plowing of the wicked, is sin.

The thoughts of the diligent tend only to plenteousness; but of every one that is hasty only to want.

The getting of treasures by a lying tongue is a vanity tossed to and fro of them that seek death.

The robbery of the wicked shall destroy them; because they refuse to do judgment.

The way of man is froward and strange:

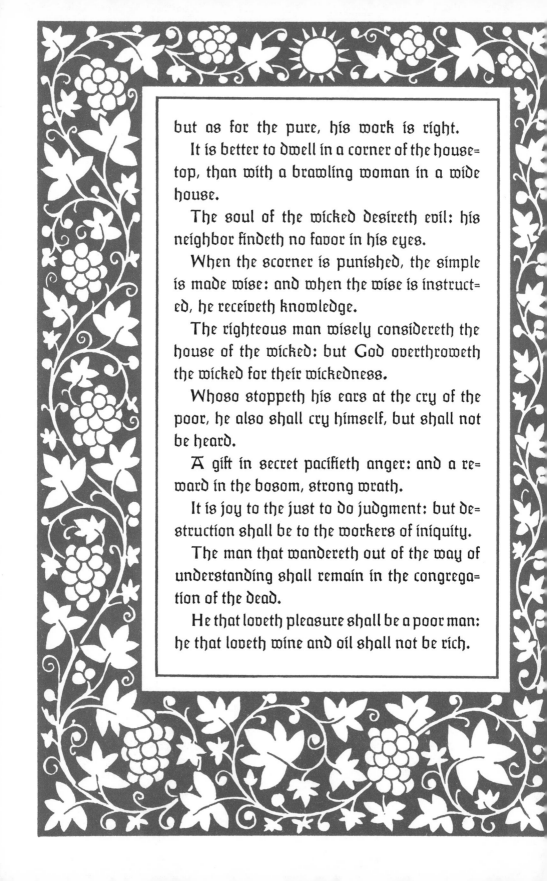

but as for the pure, his work is right.

It is better to dwell in a corner of the house=top, than with a brawling woman in a wide house.

The soul of the wicked desireth evil: his neighbor findeth no favor in his eyes.

When the scorner is punished, the simple is made wise: and when the wise is instruct=ed, he receiveth knowledge.

The righteous man wisely considereth the house of the wicked: but God overthroweth the wicked for their wickedness.

Whoso stoppeth his ears at the cry of the poor, he also shall cry himself, but shall not be heard.

A gift in secret pacifieth anger: and a re=ward in the bosom, strong wrath.

It is joy to the just to do judgment: but de=struction shall be to the workers of iniquity.

The man that wandereth out of the way of understanding shall remain in the congrega=tion of the dead.

He that loveth pleasure shall be a poor man: he that loveth wine and oil shall not be rich.

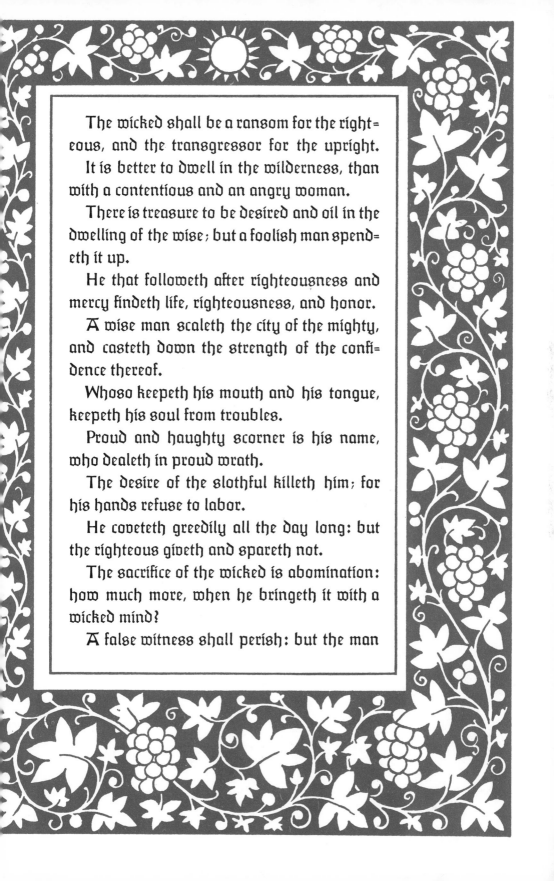

The wicked shall be a ransom for the right=
eous, and the transgressor for the upright.

It is better to dwell in the wilderness, than
with a contentious and an angry woman.

There is treasure to be desired and oil in the
dwelling of the wise; but a foolish man spend=
eth it up.

He that followeth after righteousness and
mercy findeth life, righteousness, and honor.

A wise man scaleth the city of the mighty,
and casteth down the strength of the confi=
dence thereof.

Whoso keepeth his mouth and his tongue,
keepeth his soul from troubles.

Proud and haughty scorner is his name,
who dealeth in proud wrath.

The desire of the slothful killeth him; for
his hands refuse to labor.

He coveteth greedily all the day long: but
the righteous giveth and spareth not.

The sacrifice of the wicked is abomination:
how much more, when he bringeth it with a
wicked mind?

A false witness shall perish: but the man

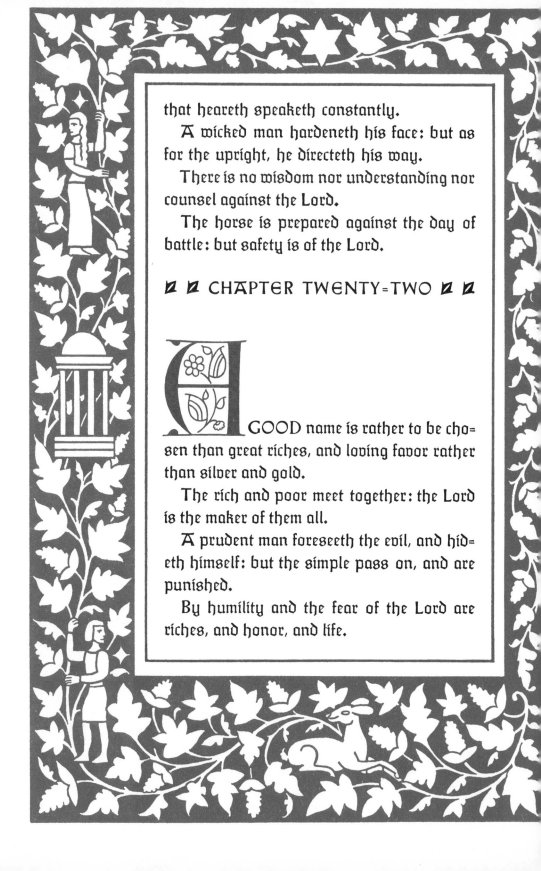

that heareth speaketh constantly.

A wicked man hardeneth his face: but as for the upright, he directeth his way.

There is no wisdom nor understanding nor counsel against the Lord.

The horse is prepared against the day of battle: but safety is of the Lord.

◪ ◪ CHAPTER TWENTY=TWO ◪ ◪

A GOOD name is rather to be cho= sen than great riches, and loving favor rather than silver and gold.

The rich and poor meet together: the Lord is the maker of them all.

A prudent man foreseeth the evil, and hid= eth himself: but the simple pass on, and are punished.

By humility and the fear of the Lord are riches, and honor, and life.

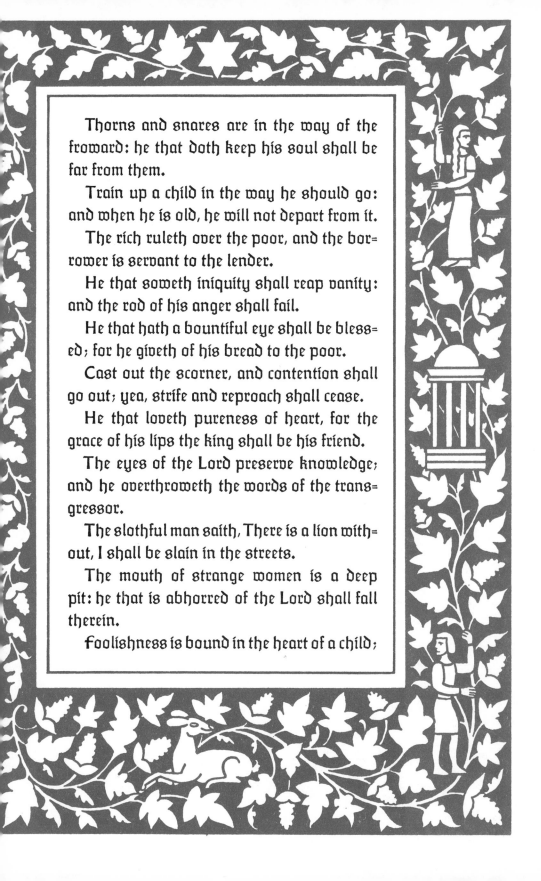

Thorns and snares are in the way of the froward: he that doth keep his soul shall be far from them.

Train up a child in the way he should go: and when he is old, he will not depart from it.

The rich ruleth over the poor, and the borrower is servant to the lender.

He that soweth iniquity shall reap vanity: and the rod of his anger shall fail.

He that hath a bountiful eye shall be blessed; for he giveth of his bread to the poor.

Cast out the scorner, and contention shall go out; yea, strife and reproach shall cease.

He that loveth pureness of heart, for the grace of his lips the king shall be his friend.

The eyes of the Lord preserve knowledge; and he overthroweth the words of the transgressor.

The slothful man saith, There is a lion without, I shall be slain in the streets.

The mouth of strange women is a deep pit: he that is abhorred of the Lord shall fall therein.

Foolishness is bound in the heart of a child;

but the rod of correction shall drive it far from him.

He that oppresseth the poor to increase his riches, and he that giveth to the rich, shall sure= ly come to want.

Bow down thine ear, and hear the words of the wise, and apply thine heart unto my knowl= edge.

For it is a pleasant thing if thou keep them within thee; they shall withal be fitted in thy lips.

That thy trust may be in the Lord, I have made known to thee this day, even to thee.

Have not I written to thee excellent things in counsels and knowledge, that I might make thee know the certainty of the words of truth; that thou mightest answer the words of truth to them that send unto thee?

Rob not the poor, because he is poor: nei= ther oppress the afflicted in the gate: for the Lord will plead their cause, and spoil the soul of those that spoiled them.

Make no friendship with an angry man; and with a furious man thou shalt not go; lest thou learn his ways, and get a snare to thy soul.

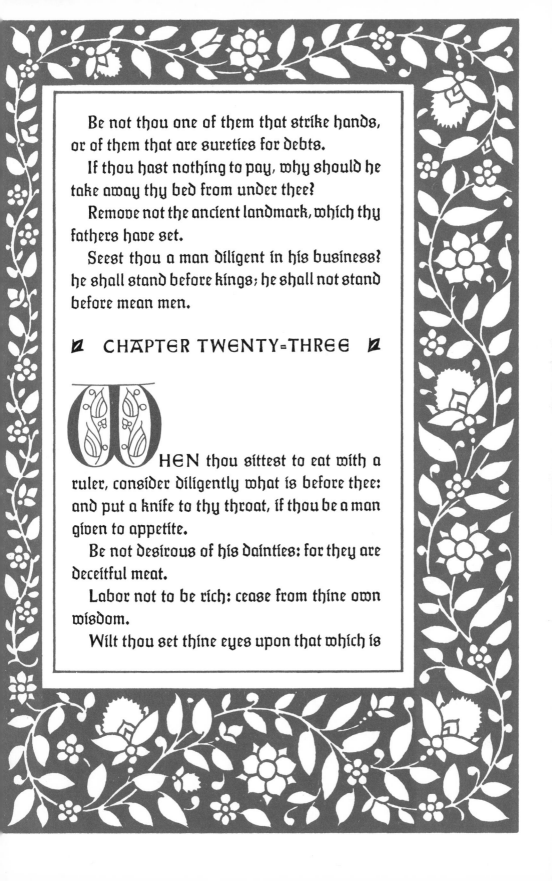

Be not thou one of them that strike hands, or of them that are sureties for debts.

If thou hast nothing to pay, why should he take away thy bed from under thee?

Remove not the ancient landmark, which thy fathers have set.

Seest thou a man diligent in his business? he shall stand before kings; he shall not stand before mean men.

CHAPTER TWENTY-THREE

WHEN thou sittest to eat with a ruler, consider diligently what is before thee: and put a knife to thy throat, if thou be a man given to appetite.

Be not desirous of his dainties: for they are deceitful meat.

Labor not to be rich: cease from thine own wisdom.

Wilt thou set thine eyes upon that which is

not? for riches certainly make themselves wings; they fly away as an eagle toward heaven.

Eat thou not the bread of him that hath an evil eye, neither desire thou his dainty meats: for as he thinketh in his heart, so is he: Eat and drink, saith he to thee; but his heart is not with thee.

The morsel which thou hast eaten shalt thou vomit up, and lose thy sweet words.

Speak not in the ears of a fool: for he will despise the wisdom of thy words.

Remove not the old landmark; and enter not into the fields of the fatherless: for their Redeemer is mighty; he shall plead their cause with thee.

Apply thine heart unto instruction, and thine ears to the words of knowledge.

Withhold not correction from the child: for if thou beatest him with the rod, he shall not die.

Thou shalt beat him with the rod, and shalt deliver his soul from hell.

My son, if thine heart be wise, my heart shall rejoice, even mine.

Yea, my reins shall rejoice, when thy lips speak right things.

Let not thine heart envy sinners; but be thou in the fear of the Lord all the day long.

For surely there is an end; and thine expectation shall not be cut off.

Hear thou, my son, and be wise, and guide thine heart in the way.

Be not among winebibbers; among riotous eaters of flesh: for the drunkard and the glutton shall come to poverty: and drowsiness shall clothe a man with rags.

Hearken unto thy father that begat thee, and despise not thy mother when she is old.

Buy the truth, and sell it not; also wisdom, and instruction, and understanding.

The father of the righteous shall greatly rejoice: and he that begetteth a wise child shall have joy of him.

Thy father and thy mother shall be glad, and she that bare thee shall rejoice.

My son, give me thine heart, and let thine eyes observe my ways.

For a whore is a deep ditch; and a strange

woman is a narrow pit.

She also lieth in wait as for a prey, and increaseth the transgressors among men.

Who hath woe? who hath sorrow? who hath contentions? who hath babbling? who hath wounds without cause? who hath redness of eyes?

They that tarry long at the wine; they that go to seek mixed wine.

Look not thou upon the wine when it is red, when it giveth his color in the cup, when it moveth itself aright.

At the last it biteth like a serpent, and stingeth like an adder.

Thine eyes shall behold strange women, and thine heart shall utter perverse things.

Yea, thou shalt be as he that lieth down in the midst of the sea, or as he that lieth upon the top of a mast.

They have stricken me, shalt thou say, and I was not sick; they have beaten me, and I felt it not: when shall I awake? I will seek it yet again.

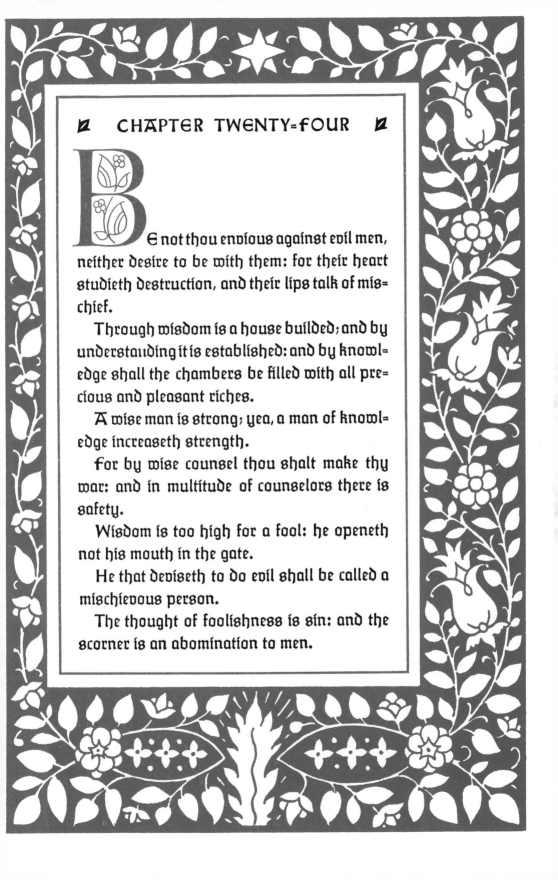

CHAPTER TWENTY=FOUR

BE not thou envious against evil men, neither desire to be with them: for their heart studieth destruction, and their lips talk of mischief.

Through wisdom is a house builded; and by understanding it is established: and by knowledge shall the chambers be filled with all precious and pleasant riches.

A wise man is strong; yea, a man of knowledge increaseth strength.

For by wise counsel thou shalt make thy war: and in multitude of counselors there is safety.

Wisdom is too high for a fool: he openeth not his mouth in the gate.

He that deviseth to do evil shall be called a mischievous person.

The thought of foolishness is sin: and the scorner is an abomination to men.

If thou faint in the day of adversity, thy strength is small.

If thou forbear to deliver them that are drawn unto death, and those that are ready to be slain; if thou sayest, Behold, we knew it not; doth not he that pondereth the heart consider it? and he that keepeth thy soul, doth not he know it? and shall not he render to every man according to his works?

My son, eat thou honey, because it is good; and the honeycomb, which is sweet to thy taste: so shall the knowledge of wisdom be unto thy soul: when thou hast found it, then there shall be a reward, and thy expectation shall not be cut off.

Lay not wait, O wicked man, against the dwelling of the righteous; spoil not his resting place: for a just man falleth seven times, and riseth up again: but the wicked shall fall into mischief.

Rejoice not when thine enemy falleth, and let not thine heart be glad when he stumbleth: lest the Lord see it, and it displease him, and he turn away his wrath from him.

Fret not thyself because of evil men, neither be thou envious at the wicked; for there shall be no reward to the evil man; the candle of the wicked shall be put out.

My son, fear thou the Lord and the king: and meddle not with them that are given to change: for their calamity shall rise suddenly; and who knoweth the ruin of them both?

These things also belong to the wise. It is not good to have respect of persons in judgment.

He that saith unto the wicked, Thou art righteous; him shall the people curse, nations shall abhor him: but to them that rebuke him shall be delight, and a good blessing shall come upon them.

Every man shall kiss his lips that giveth a right answer.

Prepare thy work without, and make it fit for thyself in the field; and afterward build thine house.

Be not a witness against thy neighbor without cause; and deceive not with thy lips.

Say not, I will do so to him as he hath done

to me: I will render to the man according to his work.

I went by the field of the slothful, and by the vineyard of the man void of understanding; and, lo, it was all grown over with thorns, and nettles had covered the face thereof, and the stone wall thereof was broken down.

Then I saw, and considered it well: I looked upon it, and received instruction.

Yet a little sleep, a little slumber, a little folding of the hands to sleep: so shall thy poverty come as one that traveleth; and thy want as an armed man.

CHAPTER TWENTY=FIVE

THESE are also proverbs of Solomon, which the men of Hezekiah king of Judah copied out.

It is the glory of God to conceal a thing: but the honor of kings is to search out a matter.

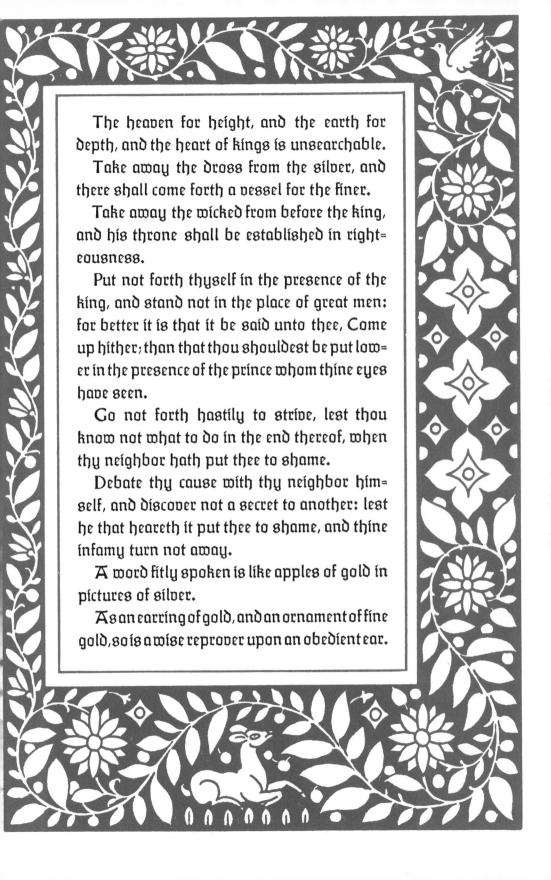

The heaven for height, and the earth for depth, and the heart of kings is unsearchable.

Take away the dross from the silver, and there shall come forth a vessel for the finer.

Take away the wicked from before the king, and his throne shall be established in right=eousness.

Put not forth thyself in the presence of the king, and stand not in the place of great men: for better it is that it be said unto thee, Come up hither; than that thou shouldest be put low=er in the presence of the prince whom thine eyes have seen.

Go not forth hastily to strive, lest thou know not what to do in the end thereof, when thy neighbor hath put thee to shame.

Debate thy cause with thy neighbor him=self, and discover not a secret to another: lest he that heareth it put thee to shame, and thine infamy turn not away.

A word fitly spoken is like apples of gold in pictures of silver.

As an earring of gold, and an ornament of fine gold, so is a wise reprover upon an obedient ear.

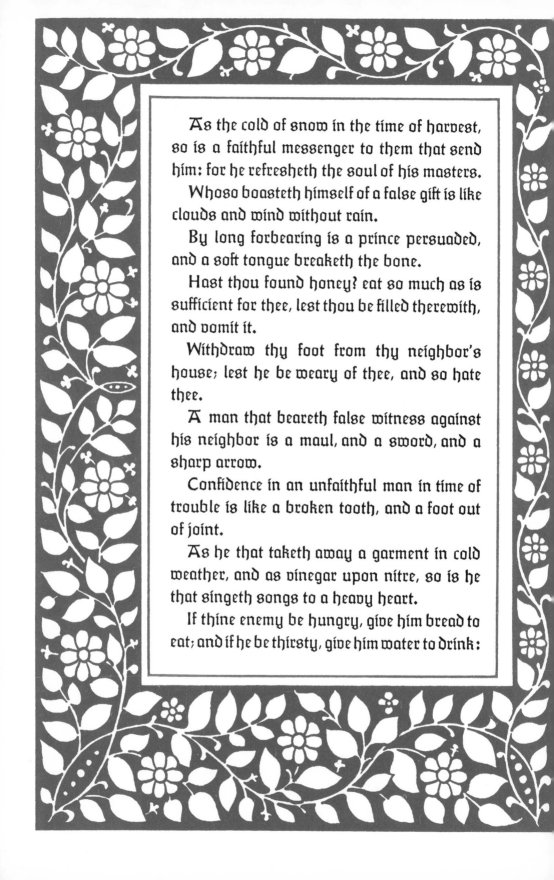

As the cold of snow in the time of harvest, so is a faithful messenger to them that send him: for he refresheth the soul of his masters.

Whoso boasteth himself of a false gift is like clouds and wind without rain.

By long forbearing is a prince persuaded, and a soft tongue breaketh the bone.

Hast thou found honey? eat so much as is sufficient for thee, lest thou be filled therewith, and vomit it.

Withdraw thy foot from thy neighbor's house; lest he be weary of thee, and so hate thee.

A man that beareth false witness against his neighbor is a maul, and a sword, and a sharp arrow.

Confidence in an unfaithful man in time of trouble is like a broken tooth, and a foot out of joint.

As he that taketh away a garment in cold weather, and as vinegar upon nitre, so is he that singeth songs to a heavy heart.

If thine enemy be hungry, give him bread to eat; and if he be thirsty, give him water to drink:

for thou shalt heap coals of fire upon his head, and the Lord shall reward thee.

The north wind driveth away rain: so doth an angry countenance a backbiting tongue.

It is better to dwell in the corner of the housetop, than with a brawling woman and in a wide house.

As cold waters to a thirsty soul, so is good news from a far country.

A righteous man falling down before the wicked is as a troubled fountain, and a corrupt spring.

It is not good to eat much honey: so for men to search their own glory is not glory.

He that hath no rule over his own spirit is like a city that is broken down, and without walls.

☙ ☙ CHAPTER TWENTY-SIX ☙ ☙

AS snow in summer, and as rain in harvest, so honor is not seemly for a fool.

As the bird by wandering, as the swallow

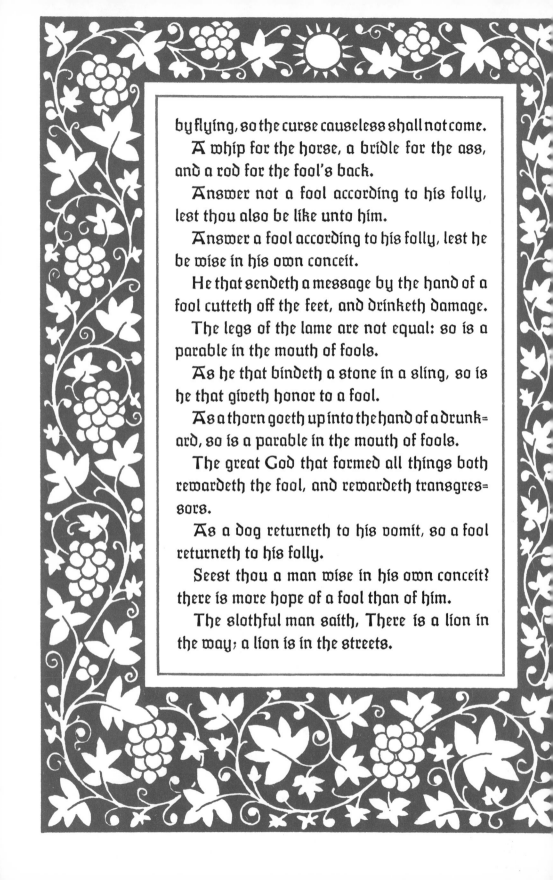

by flying, so the curse causeless shall not come.

A whip for the horse, a bridle for the ass, and a rod for the fool's back.

Answer not a fool according to his folly, lest thou also be like unto him.

Answer a fool according to his folly, lest he be wise in his own conceit.

He that sendeth a message by the hand of a fool cutteth off the feet, and drinketh damage.

The legs of the lame are not equal: so is a parable in the mouth of fools.

As he that bindeth a stone in a sling, so is he that giveth honor to a fool.

As a thorn goeth up into the hand of a drunk= ard, so is a parable in the mouth of fools.

The great God that formed all things both rewardeth the fool, and rewardeth transgres= sors.

As a dog returneth to his vomit, so a fool returneth to his folly.

Seest thou a man wise in his own conceit? there is more hope of a fool than of him.

The slothful man saith, There is a lion in the way; a lion is in the streets.

As the door turneth upon his hinges, so doth the slothful upon his bed.

The slothful hideth his hand in his bosom; it grieveth him to bring it again to his mouth.

The sluggard is wiser in his own conceit than seven men that can render a reason.

He that passeth by, and meddleth with strife belonging not to him, is like one that taketh a dog by the ears.

As a mad man who casteth firebrands, arrows, and death, so is the man that deceiveth his neighbor, and saith, Am not I in sport?

Where no wood is, there the fire goeth out: so where there is no talebearer, the strife ceaseth.

As coals are to burning coals, and wood to fire; so is a contentious man to kindle strife.

The words of a talebearer are as wounds, and they go down into the innermost parts of the belly.

Burning lips and a wicked heart are like a potsherd covered with silver dross.

He that hateth dissembleth with his lips, and layeth up deceit within him; when he speaketh fair, believe him not: for there are

seven abominations in his heart.

Whose hatred is covered by deceit, his wick=
edness shall be showed before the whole con=
gregation.

Whoso diggeth a pit shall fall therein: and
he that rolleth a stone, it will return upon him.

A lying tongue hateth those that are afflict=
ed by it; and a flattering mouth worketh ruin.

CHAPTER TWENTY=SEVEN

BOAST not thyself of to=morrow; for
thou knowest not what a day may bring forth.

Let another man praise thee, and not thine
own mouth; a stranger, and not thine own lips.

A stone is heavy, and the sand weighty; but
a fool's wrath is heavier than them both.

Wrath is cruel, and anger is outrageous; but
who is able to stand before envy?

Open rebuke is better than secret love.

Faithful are the wounds of a friend; but
the kisses of an enemy are deceitful.

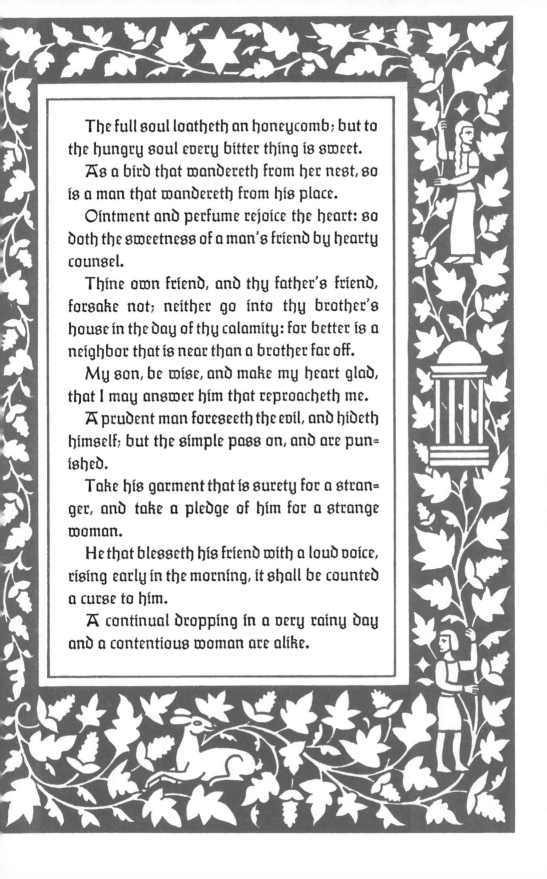

The full soul loatheth an honeycomb; but to the hungry soul every bitter thing is sweet.

As a bird that wandereth from her nest, so is a man that wandereth from his place.

Ointment and perfume rejoice the heart: so doth the sweetness of a man's friend by hearty counsel.

Thine own friend, and thy father's friend, forsake not; neither go into thy brother's house in the day of thy calamity: for better is a neighbor that is near than a brother far off.

My son, be wise, and make my heart glad, that I may answer him that reproacheth me.

A prudent man foreseeth the evil, and hideth himself; but the simple pass on, and are pun=ished.

Take his garment that is surety for a stran=ger, and take a pledge of him for a strange woman.

He that blesseth his friend with a loud voice, rising early in the morning, it shall be counted a curse to him.

A continual dropping in a very rainy day and a contentious woman are alike.

Whosoever hideth her hideth the wind, and the ointment of his right hand, which bewray=eth itself.

Iron sharpeneth iron; so a man sharpeneth the countenance of his friend.

Whoso keepeth the fig tree shall eat the fruit thereof: so he that waiteth on his master shall be honored.

As in water face answereth to face, so the heart of man to man.

Hell and destruction are never full; so the eyes of man are never satisfied.

As the fining pot for silver, and the furnace for gold; so is a man to his praise.

Though thou shouldest bray a fool in a mor=tar among wheat with a pestle, yet will not his foolishness depart from him.

Be thou diligent to know the state of thy flocks, and look well to thy herds: for riches are not for ever: and doth the crown endure to every generation?

The hay appeareth, and the tender grass showeth itself, and herbs of the mountains are gathered.

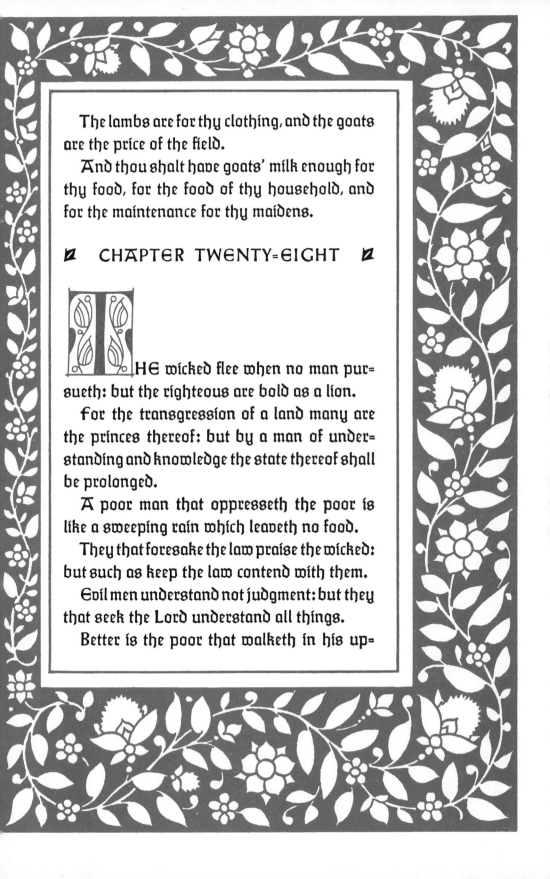

The lambs are for thy clothing, and the goats are the price of the field.

And thou shalt have goats' milk enough for thy food, for the food of thy household, and for the maintenance for thy maidens.

CHAPTER TWENTY=EIGHT

THE wicked flee when no man pur=sueth: but the righteous are bold as a lion.

For the transgression of a land many are the princes thereof: but by a man of under=standing and knowledge the state thereof shall be prolonged.

A poor man that oppresseth the poor is like a sweeping rain which leaveth no food.

They that forsake the law praise the wicked: but such as keep the law contend with them.

Evil men understand not judgment: but they that seek the Lord understand all things.

Better is the poor that walketh in his up=

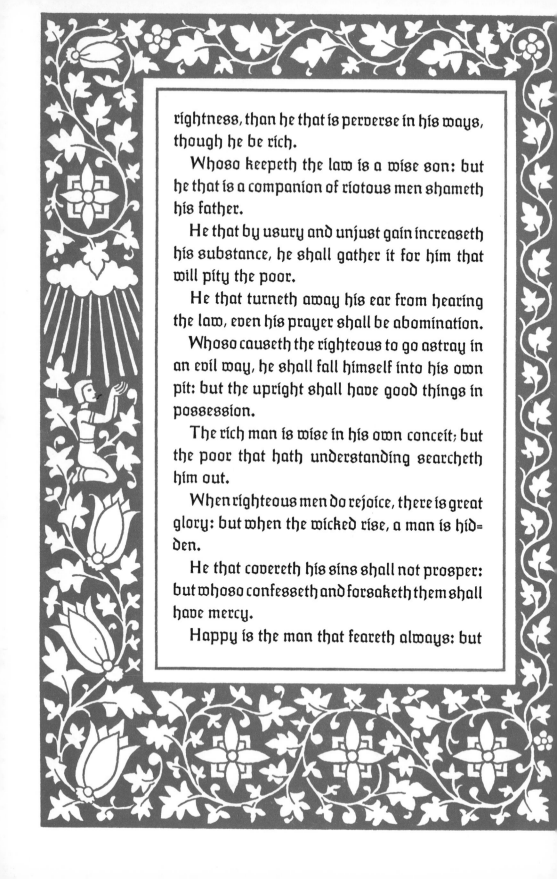

rightness, than he that is perverse in his ways, though he be rich.

Whoso keepeth the law is a wise son: but he that is a companion of riotous men shameth his father.

He that by usury and unjust gain increaseth his substance, he shall gather it for him that will pity the poor.

He that turneth away his ear from hearing the law, even his prayer shall be abomination.

Whoso causeth the righteous to go astray in an evil way, he shall fall himself into his own pit: but the upright shall have good things in possession.

The rich man is wise in his own conceit; but the poor that hath understanding searcheth him out.

When righteous men do rejoice, there is great glory: but when the wicked rise, a man is hid=den.

He that covereth his sins shall not prosper: but whoso confesseth and forsaketh them shall have mercy.

Happy is the man that feareth always: but

he that hardeneth his heart shall fall into mis=
chief.

As a roaring lion, and a ranging bear; so is
a wicked ruler over the poor people.

The prince that wanteth understanding is
also a great oppressor: but he that hateth cov=
etousness shall prolong his days.

A man that doeth violence to the blood of
any person shall flee to the pit; let no man
stay him.

Whoso walketh uprightly shall be saved:
but he that is perverse in his ways shall fall
at once.

He that tilleth his land shall have plenty of
bread: but he that followeth after vain persons
shall have poverty enough.

A faithful man shall abound with blessings:
but he that maketh haste to be rich shall not
be innocent.

To have respect of persons is not good: for,
for a piece of bread that man will transgress.

He that hasteth to be rich hath an evil eye,
and considereth not that poverty shall come
upon him.

He that rebuketh a man, afterward shall find more favor than he that flattereth with the tongue.

Whoso robbeth his father or his mother, and saith, It is no transgression; the same is the companion of a destroyer.

He that is of a proud heart stirreth up strife: but he that putteth his trust in the Lord shall be made fat.

He that trusteth in his own heart is a fool: but whoso walketh wisely, he shall be delivered.

He that giveth unto the poor shall not lack: but he that hideth his eyes shall have many a curse.

When the wicked rise, men hide themselves: but when they perish, the righteous increase.

CHAPTER TWENTY=NINE

HE, that being often reproved hardeneth his neck, shall suddenly be destroyed, and that without remedy.

When the righteous are in authority, the people rejoice: but when the wicked beareth rule, the people mourn.

Whoso loveth wisdom rejoiceth his father: but he that keepeth company with harlots spendeth his substance.

The king by judgment establisheth the land: but he that receiveth gifts overthroweth it.

A man that flattereth his neighbor spread=eth a net for his feet.

In the transgression of an evil man there is a snare: but the righteous doth sing and rejoice.

The righteous considereth the cause of the poor: but the wicked regardeth not to know it.

Scornful men bring a city into a snare: but wise men turn away wrath.

If a wise man contendeth with a foolish man, whether he rage or laugh, there is no rest.

The bloodthirsty hate the upright: but the just seek his soul.

A fool uttereth all his mind: but a wise man keepeth it in till afterward.

If a ruler hearken to lies, all his servants are wicked.

The poor and the deceitful man meet to=
gether: the Lord lighteneth both their eyes.

The king that faithfully judgeth the poor,
his throne shall be established for ever.

The rod and reproof give wisdom: but a child
left to himself bringeth his mother to shame.

When the wicked are multiplied, transgres=
sion increaseth: but the righteous shall see
their fall.

Correct thy son, and he shall give thee rest;
yea, he shall give delight unto thy soul.

Where there is no vision, the people perish:
but he that keepeth the law, happy is he.

A servant will not be corrected by words:
for though he understand he will not answer.

Seest thou a man that is hasty in his words?
there is more hope of a fool than of him.

He that delicately bringeth up his servant
from a child shall have him become his son at
the length.

An angry man stirreth up strife, and a furi=
ous man aboundeth in transgression.

A man's pride shall bring him low: but hon=
or shall uphold the humble in spirit.

Whoso is partner with a thief hateth his own soul: he heareth cursing, and bewrayeth it not.

The fear of man bringeth a snare: but who=so putteth his trust in the Lord shall be safe.

Many seek the ruler's favor; but every man's judgment cometh from the Lord.

An unjust man is an abomination to the just: and he that is upright in the way is abomination to the wicked.

◢ ◢ ◢ CHAPTER THIRTY ◢ ◢ ◢

THE words of Agur the son of Jakeh, even the prophecy: the man spake unto Ithiel, even unto Ithiel and Ucal, Surely I am more brutish than any man, and have not the un=derstanding of a man.

I neither learned wisdom, nor have the knowl=edge of the holy.

Who hath ascended up into heaven, or de=scended? who hath gathered the wind in his

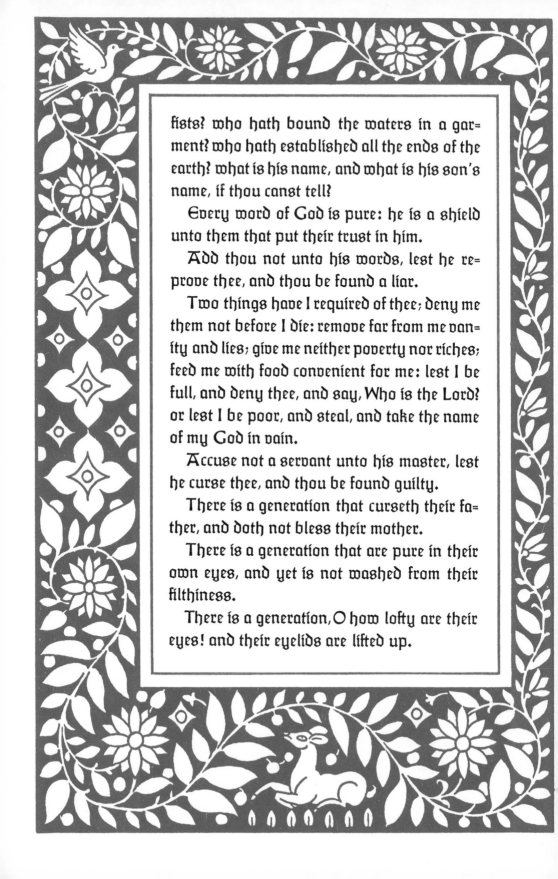

fists? who hath bound the waters in a gar=
ment? who hath established all the ends of the
earth? what is his name, and what is his son's
name, if thou canst tell?

Every word of God is pure: he is a shield
unto them that put their trust in him.

Add thou not unto his words, lest he re=
prove thee, and thou be found a liar.

Two things have I required of thee; deny me
them not before I die: remove far from me van=
ity and lies; give me neither poverty nor riches;
feed me with food convenient for me: lest I be
full, and deny thee, and say, Who is the Lord?
or lest I be poor, and steal, and take the name
of my God in vain.

Accuse not a servant unto his master, lest
he curse thee, and thou be found guilty.

There is a generation that curseth their fa=
ther, and doth not bless their mother.

There is a generation that are pure in their
own eyes, and yet is not washed from their
filthiness.

There is a generation, O how lofty are their
eyes! and their eyelids are lifted up.

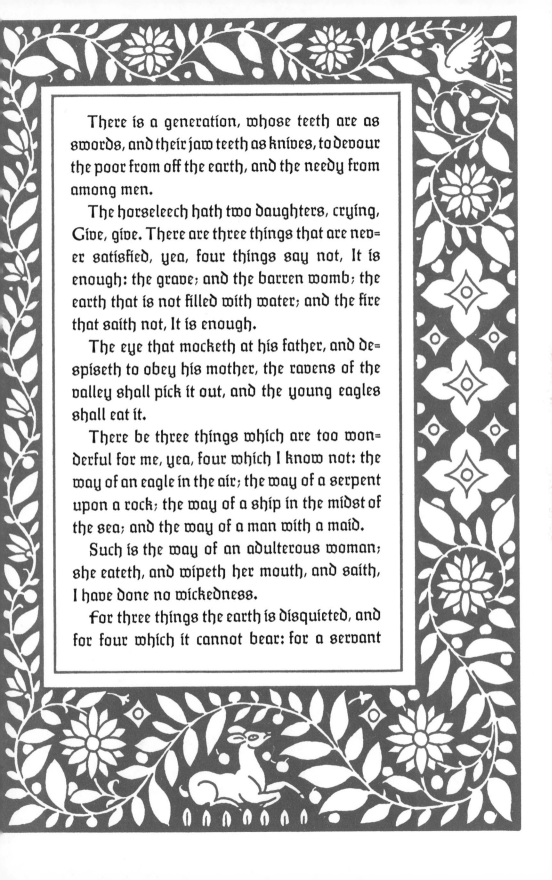

There is a generation, whose teeth are as swords, and their jaw teeth as knives, to devour the poor from off the earth, and the needy from among men.

The horseleech hath two daughters, crying, Give, give. There are three things that are nev= er satisfied, yea, four things say not, It is enough: the grave; and the barren womb; the earth that is not filled with water; and the fire that saith not, It is enough.

The eye that mocketh at his father, and de= spiseth to obey his mother, the ravens of the valley shall pick it out, and the young eagles shall eat it.

There be three things which are too won= derful for me, yea, four which I know not: the way of an eagle in the air; the way of a serpent upon a rock; the way of a ship in the midst of the sea; and the way of a man with a maid.

Such is the way of an adulterous woman; she eateth, and wipeth her mouth, and saith, I have done no wickedness.

For three things the earth is disquieted, and for four which it cannot bear: for a servant

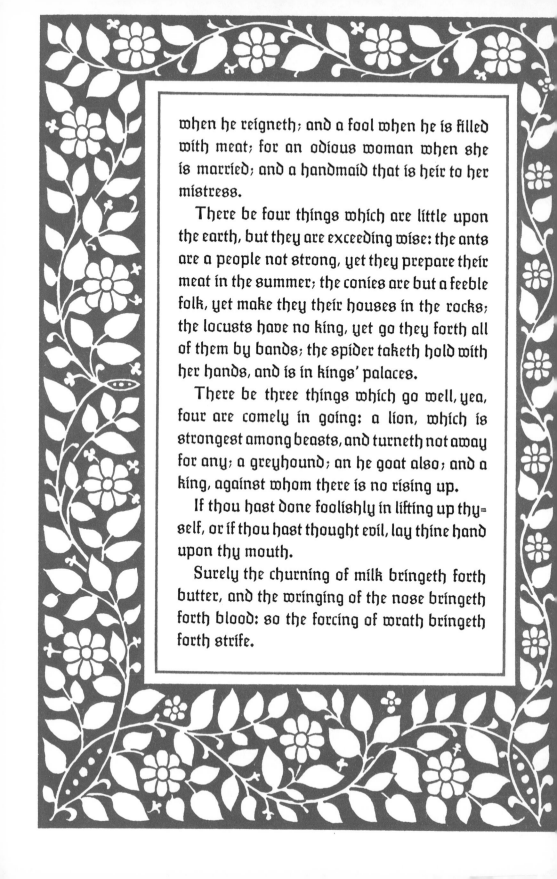

when he reigneth; and a fool when he is filled
with meat; for an odious woman when she
is married; and a handmaid that is heir to her
mistress.

There be four things which are little upon
the earth, but they are exceeding wise: the ants
are a people not strong, yet they prepare their
meat in the summer; the conies are but a feeble
folk, yet make they their houses in the rocks;
the locusts have no king, yet go they forth all
of them by bands; the spider taketh hold with
her hands, and is in kings' palaces.

There be three things which go well, yea,
four are comely in going: a lion, which is
strongest among beasts, and turneth not away
for any; a greyhound; an he goat also; and a
king, against whom there is no rising up.

If thou hast done foolishly in lifting up thy=
self, or if thou hast thought evil, lay thine hand
upon thy mouth.

Surely the churning of milk bringeth forth
butter, and the wringing of the nose bringeth
forth blood: so the forcing of wrath bringeth
forth strife.

CHAPTER THIRTY-ONE

THE words of king Lemuel, the prophecy that his mother taught him.

What, my son? and what, the son of my womb? and what, the son of my vows?

Give not thy strength unto women, nor thy ways to that which destroyeth kings.

It is not for kings, O Lemuel, it is not for kings to drink wine; nor for princes strong drink: lest they drink, and forget the law, and pervert the judgment of any of the afflicted.

Give strong drink unto him that is ready to perish, and wine unto those that be of heavy hearts.

Let him drink, and forget his poverty, and remember his misery no more.

Open thy mouth for the dumb in the cause of all such as are appointed to destruction.

Open thy mouth, judge righteously, and plead the cause of the poor and needy.

Who can find a virtuous woman? for her price is far above rubies.

The heart of her husband doth safely trust in her, so that he shall have no need of spoil.

She will do him good and not evil all the days of her life.

She seeketh wool, and flax, and worketh willingly with her hands.

She is like the merchants' ships; she bringeth her food from afar.

She riseth also while it is yet night, and giveth meat to her household and a portion to her maidens.

She considereth a field, and buyeth it: with the fruit of her hands she planteth a vineyard.

She girdeth her loins with strength, and strengtheneth her arms.

She perceiveth that her merchandise is good: her candle goeth not out by night.

She layeth her hands to the spindle, and her hands hold the distaff.

She stretcheth out her hand to the poor; yea, she reacheth forth her hands to the needy.

She is not afraid of the snow for her house=

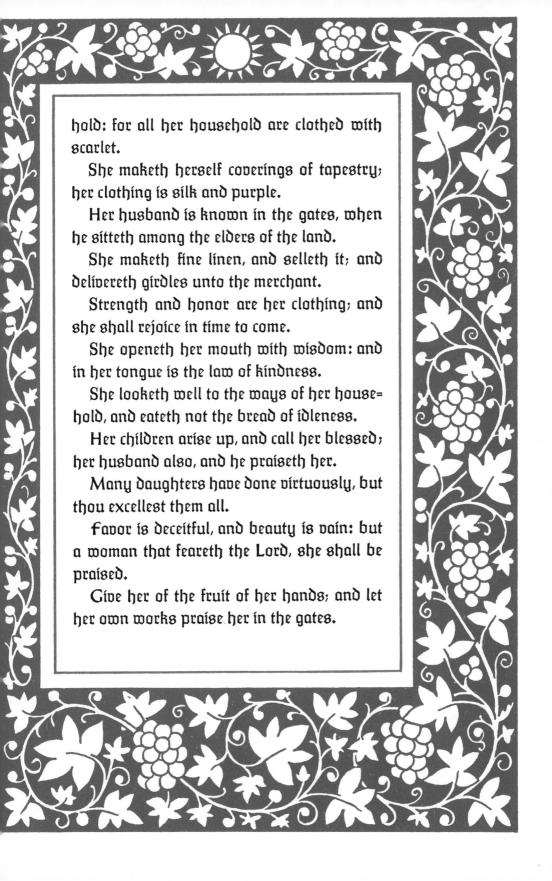

hold: for all her household are clothed with scarlet.

She maketh herself coverings of tapestry; her clothing is silk and purple.

Her husband is known in the gates, when he sitteth among the elders of the land.

She maketh fine linen, and selleth it; and delivereth girdles unto the merchant.

Strength and honor are her clothing; and she shall rejoice in time to come.

She openeth her mouth with wisdom: and in her tongue is the law of kindness.

She looketh well to the ways of her house=hold, and eateth not the bread of idleness.

Her children arise up, and call her blessed; her husband also, and he praiseth her.

Many daughters have done virtuously, but thou excellest them all.

Favor is deceitful, and beauty is vain: but a woman that feareth the Lord, she shall be praised.

Give her of the fruit of her hands; and let her own works praise her in the gates.

For this edition of The Book of Proverbs the
translation has been taken from that of the
Holy Bible prepared at the command of King
James I of England and first set forth in
the year 1611. The book was decorated
by Valenti Angelo, who also
set the text by hand.